DEEP IN THE HEART OF TEXAS

DEEP IN THE HEART OF TEXAS

TEXAS RANCHERS IN THEIR OWN WORDS

PHOTOGRAPHED AND PRODUCED BY KATHLEEN JO RYAN

DESIGN BY TOM MORGAN

A CF RANCH BOOK

TEN SPEED PRESS
Berkeley, California

TO ALL TEXAS RANCHERS — THE HEART OF TEXAS

Introduction, text, and photographs © 1999 Kathleen Jo Ryan

A CF Ranch Book
CF Publishing, LLC
Fort Worth, Texas 76107

TEN SPEED PRESS
P.O. Box 7123
Berkeley, California 94707
www.tenspeed.com

Distributed in Australia by Simon and Schuster Australia, in Canada by Ten Speed Press Canada, in New Zealand by Tandem Press, in South Africa by Real Books, in Southeast Asia by Berkeley Books, and in the United Kingdom and Europe by Airlift Books.

Concept and design: Tom Morgan, Blue Design (www.bluedes.com)
Editorial supervisor: Kathleen Jo Ryan
Project supervisor: Heidi Hause

Library of Congress Cataloging-in-Publication Data
Ryan, Kathleen Jo, 1946-
    Deep in the heart of Texas ranching / photography & text by Kathleen Jo Ryan.
      p.   cm.
    ISBN 1-58008-101-0 (pbk.)
    1. Ranching—Texas.   2. Ranch life—Texas.   3. Beef cattle—Texas.   4. Ranchers—Texas—
Interviews.   5. Texas—Biography.   6. Ranching—Texas—Pictorial works.   7. Ranch life—
Texas—Pictorial works .
I. Title.
SF196.u5R93   1999
636.2'01'0922764—dc21   99-11726
                                                                     CIP

First printing, 1999
Printed in China

1 2 3 4 5 6 7 8 9 10 — 03 02 01 00 99

CONTENTS

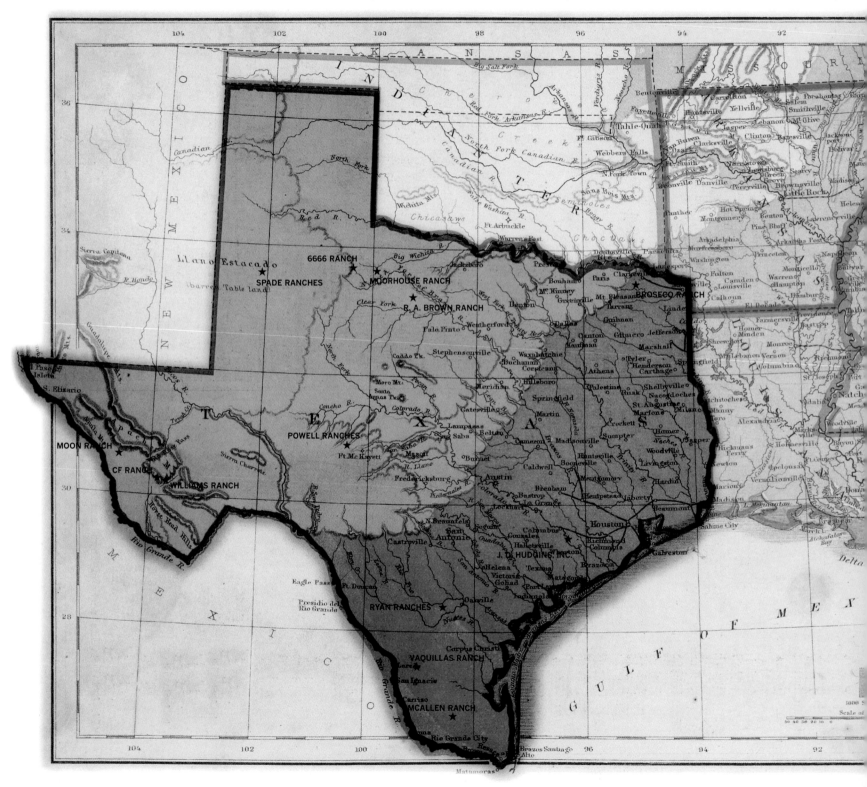

Introduction

Kathleen Jo Ryan

It is my last morning on a Texas ranch for a while. At sunrise I am waiting for the cowboys to gather cattle and bring them to the pens. The light is just dawning from the East with fine brushstrokes of pink, peach and amber light streaking across a vast blue horizon. I twirl around. As always I am captivated by this singular Texas horizon. Does the West seem bigger with this three-hundred-sixty degree openness or with mountains dotted somewhere on the horizon?

From my perch on a West Texas bluff I imagine seeing forever. Very still, only morning sounds — the birds are busy. I sigh. It feels familiar yet so foreign. It's Texas, not Wyoming or Nevada where I am most at home — this feels desolate but not isolated. Shadows from telephone lines fall across a dirt road. I am suddenly reminded; it is only thirty minutes to a twenty-four hour convenience store. Reality?

Since 1974, I have photographically documented ranching in the American West. As a westerner, born and bred, I have driven over five-hundred thousand miles crisscrossing the western states. From 1986 through 1989, I photographed and produced my second book, *Ranching Traditions: Legacy of the American West*. In October 1997, Al Micallef, rancher, entrepreneur and restaurateur, approached me with his vision to produce a beautiful celebration of Texas ranching today. The result is *Texas Cattle Barons: Their Families, Land and Legacy*. This is the companion book.

To produce *Texas Cattle Barons*, I interviewed ranchers while photographing the thirteen Texas ranches we had selected. The widely acclaimed Texas writer Elmer Kelton agreed to write essays profiling each ranch from the transcripts of these interviews. The result was an abundance of information, much more than could be included in their profiles. We realized that this substantial content warranted a separate book. The interview transcripts were edited and condensed for readability. We have included questions that served as a guide to provoke thought and conversation. To preserve the spontaneous nature of these personal interviews this book retains the question and answer format from the original conversations — truly *Texas ranchers in their own words*.

This book is a clear demonstration that substance and truth are more powerful than myth. These ranchers reveal through their own words the depth of their character, the sophistication of their businesses and a devoted commitment to serve as stewards of wildlife, land and livestock. They are the guardians of the remaining open spaces in the American West while providing nutritious food and fiber for society. They are a living link with our past, often an actual part of Texas history. They may inspire us to return to traditional values.

Ranching by its very nature is set in an unpredictable, unforgiving and sometimes isolated and brutal environment. Competence and courage emerge from the demands and hardship imposed by this life. Today ranchers exemplify these qualities; they embody values we seek, such as self-reliance, morality and decency. These interviews invite the reader beyond the ranch gate and into each home to share in the thoughtful efforts by each rancher to offer insights into their lives.

In retrospect this year was a pivotal year to portray ranching in Texas. First, it was a disastrous year — smoke blanketed the state from fires in Mexico, statewide drought, extreme temperatures and severe rains resulted in devastating floods — threatening all agriculture. Besides the Texas crises were other cultural factors affecting ranchers: cattle prices continued to be ridiculously low; the consumer's image of beef remained negatively influenced by popular myth; expanding govern-

mental intrusion and regulatory encroachment and the momentum of growing
estrangement between consumers and agriculture.

These influences are attacking the heart of agriculture today, especially ranching —
weakening and eroding its foundation. In spite of hardships, my ranching friends have
always voiced an eternal optimism — a brightness of the future for the current and
following generations. This past year, 1998, was different. There was still an attitude
"tomorrow will be better" or "next spring it will improve" underlying whatever the crisis.
But for the first time I heard generational ranchers discuss concern for their offspring's
willingness to continue to ranch. Now, it is no longer assumed that a ranch will pass
onto the next generation. No longer is there a sense of obligation that a younger generation will or should automatically follow the traditions of the three or four generations that
preceeded them.

The concern for the future of ranching is now discussed in the context of making
economic sense. There is still a longing to carry on the historic tradition of previous
generations, but it is tempered with modern realities. Ranchers do not want to saddle
their offspring with the burden of tradition if the ranch can not make it financially. Family
ranchers today are sending their children off to school, encouraging them to sample life
away from their ranching traditions. Once they have tasted life and are still committed to
ranch they are welcome to continue tradition. If not, they are being encouraged to
navigate new paths. Their choices will form a critical crossroads for our culture.

Ranching in Texas and throughout the western states forms an infrastructure that
holds together the fabric of rural America and the American West. If ranchers are
displaced we unravel the heart of the American West — environmentally, economically
and culturally. The implications for our predominantly urban culture, should the younger
generation decide not to pursue the family ranching tradition, are sobering. For starters,
the ranch will be sold. Land and water rights, being the greatest assets, will be sold to the
highest bidders, not necessarily the best stewards. Already evident are situations of

unconscious or greedy development leaving environmental voids in the heart of our American West. Water rights sold down river never return to their homeland. The loss of tax revenues supporting small rural communities threatens their very existence.

Fortunately so far, the ranchers portrayed in this book are continuing their tradition with hopes for a better tomorrow. I invite you to open your mind and heart to these individuals. It is still their earnest desire to continue to improve life — not only for themselves and their families, but also for their communities — local and global. May their own words inform and enlighten you. After all these years I continue to be an even more devoted admirer — they are the most chivalrous and courageous people to grace my life.

On my last night in Texas the sun sets, a fiery amber ball dropping into a sea of brush and mesquite. These ranchers hold our American West in their hands and I pray we encourage them to continue.

The following are sample questions that I used as a guide and trigger for provoking thoughts and dialogue:

- How old is your ranch? When was it founded and by whom?

- Has it grown through the years, and if so, how, and how much?

- What changes has your operation undergone since the earliest days? What has been tried and found to work? What has been tried and found *not* to work?

- What are the factors that make your ranch successful today? What have been the obstacles and how have they been overcome? Any obstacles that have *not* been overcome?

- What is the personal participation of individuals in your daily operation, and in the planning? Husband? Wife? Children? Other relatives? Is the next generation in line to continue the operation?

- Do you have extra outside help that participate in the daily operation? How long have they been involved? How do they participate? What is their level of responsibility?

- How much has outside income figured into your operation? Minerals? Profession?

- Are there peculiarities that pertain to this specific place, specific environment, that have required special adaptations? How have these either favored your operation or challenged it? (climate, topography, vegetation, water, etc.)

- What innovations have you introduced to improve your operation? Are any of these innovations applicable to the industry as a whole? What impact do your innovations have on the land, livestock, wildlife?

- How is your operation preparing for the new century? If money or labor were not a consideration what vision would you have for your ranch?

- What do you see for the future of your ranch operation? What do you see as the future for the ranching industry as a whole?

- What legacy do you want to leave for the future generations? How would you like others to view your ranching operation?

Broseco Ranch

Interview with Tom Woodward, manager, Broseco Ranch, at his home ranch in Decatur, Texas on June 12, 1998. Broseco and its holding company, Broventure are owned by the Brown family. Phil English is the President and CEO, and his wife Deb is a descendent of Donaldson Brown, the company's founder.

KJR: Is there a difference in the ranching culture of East Texas?

TW: One of the differences for example, in West Texas, there's a process known as neighboring. When you're getting ready to work cattle neighboring ranchers will come and be involved — you spend two or three days working your cattle and then you go help them work their cattle. That doesn't occur in East Texas because most of the cattle in East Texas are on very small operations. The Broseco is the largest ranching operation east of I-35.

KJR: So how do you work cattle differently?

TW: We find a few "day labor" cowboys to come in when we're doing cattle work. We have a state-of-the-art set of working pens and our guys can put a herd of 300 cows and 300 calves in the pens and have them worked before lunch. Our philosophy is to put as little stress on cattle as possible, get it done as quickly as possible, and get the cattle back together and out of the pens. When they're working calves, they can work one every

35 or 40 seconds. The calf receives minimum stress. He doesn't miss his mama very long.

KJR: What makes the Broseco ranch successful today?

TW: What has helped us to move forward is our production system and economics of production. How you handle calves at weaning time is a major consideration and we have our own program for preconditioning our calves at the ranch. We sort calves that are big enough at weaning and send some to the feed lot. The balance of the calves will either run on cool season grasses in East Texas, moved out to wheat country, or go to the rolling plains or on to the panhandle. We haven't sold any calves off the cow now for probably six or seven years. We retain and precondition every calf.

KJR: Would you describe precondition?

TW: Preconditioning is the whole process of getting that calf weaned off of the cow and building his immunity. We sort the calves from the cows and put them through the chutes for a respiratory shot. Then they go straight to the weaning pen. A weaned calf wants to walk the fence and try to get out and go back to its mother. We put someone on foot in the weaning pen with them and try to control their movement to stop the walking process. We take the stress off the calves, get them thinking about something other than the mother they just lost. Next is fresh water, hay and a small amount of feed for 48 hours. Then we take those calves, very carefully, out of the pens and into traps to watch them until they start eating grass. We come back in a couple of weeks and give the respiratory booster and the other vaccines that they need. Management of these calves at weaning is a big factor — reducing the stress and boosting their immune system. We have very few health problems with them as they go to pasture or the feedlot.

KJR: What are your goals for the ranch?

TW: Basically, we're attempting to retain ownership of our calves through the feed lot, and even to the rail in a lot of instances. We want to focus more on the right genetics. We want data coming back to us, telling us if we are doing it right or not and then to make the adjustments needed. We breed our heifers to calve at two and then they have to be bred every fall or they don't stay at Broseco Ranch. We focus on maternal characteristics. A cow must breed and have the ability to survive in our climate. The calf must perform the rest of the way through the system. I think all cattlemen are beginning to realize that we're in the food business. If we don't produce a product that the consumer wants, this wonderful heritage and all that we enjoy could be in the past.

TW: This is a business and we have to make money to stay in it. As the younger generations start becoming owners of the land that their grandfathers and their fathers have operated for all these years, they want to know what the return on investment is for their operation. If they inherited a large ranch and can pay the inheritance taxes, then maybe it can continue to operate. As a business, the return on investment in the ranching business has never been very good. So, we keep trying to improve our position to make a better return.

KJR: Can you describe other innovations?

TW: One of the things we looked at in the '80's was our grazing system. We had to grow more grass. The cattle were spot grazing. You'd find a place where it was grazed to the ground and right next to it would be grass a foot tall. How do you manage cattle so that they don't do that? Once that big spot of mature grass gets there, it's not very palatable. We're in tall grass country with low quality forage grasses, and once they mature it's very difficult to get cattle to consume them. You've heard the old saying, "you can go to East Texas and see cattle belly-deep in grass starving to death," and that's true. It's totally different from short-grass country. There are many low quality grasses that will grow fast

and get up belly high to a cow but the cow won't eat them. She'll walk through it and literally starve to death because it's so unpalatable. So we started developing an intensive grazing system.

KJR: Was this the Holistic Resource Management philosophy?

TW: We went to the HRM School, to Parson's School, and adopted a combination of thoughts from their schools and our own experience. It made us refocus on what we're trying to do. What's our objective, what are our goals? Holistic Resource Management tries to take all your resources and look at them as a whole, and then manage them as a whole. To optimize, not only production but also the aesthetic value of the property, the culture and the family, all of the components. I wanted to figure out how to graze those pastures to stop some spot grazing and get a better utilization of the grass. We were able to raise our production level by using an intensive grazing system. The pounds of calf weaned per acre were 34% greater than we got on continuously grazed pastures.

KJR: How often do you rotate them?

TW: Anywhere from daily to weekly. That is a management decision based on what the grass is doing, environment, rainfall, how the cattle are handling that kind of grass. It's a different set of problems than you have in the more arid climates. Time controlled grazing is really what it is. It's not how often you rotate, or how many cattle; it's how you control the time that they're on a particular area while giving another area rest. As you get into higher rainfall climates, it is more intensive. You have to watch very closely, if you graze a paddock one day too long, then you can damage the pasture and hurt your cattle performance. This makes for more intensive management.

KJR: Do you use electrical fence?

TW: Yes, because I could not afford to build that many miles of permanent fence. Where it was costing $5,000 a mile to build a permanent fence, I could build a mile electric for

$600.00. We used one strand of electric wire. It's a psychological barrier. The cattle know when it's hot and when it is not. Once they learn the system, it's no problem. You must continually check it to be sure its running at the right voltage and that all your fences are hot. You'll always have brush growing up in it; grass growing up in it; insulators that give way. I haven't run into a cowboy yet that likes electric fences, but it's the only way we can economically take a larger pasture and break it into a bunch of smaller paddocks. If you're going to do intensive grazing, you're probably going to have to look at some type of electric fence.

KJR: How do you manage your people?
TW: People management is an important issue. We have adopted a system where the land and livestock are divided up into four units. Each unit has a foreman with an assistant and they take care of around two thousand head of cattle. They have the responsibility and the opportunity to make some decisions on their own: how they manage their grazing, where they move their cattle, how they maintain their fences and water and how they take care of the mineral supplementation and feeding of their cattle. Giving employees an opportunity to be involved in the management, having a feedback system and having a way to evaluate their performance seems to be positive for the ranch

KJR: Is there a bonus system?
TW: Yes. We establish annual goals for each unit and evaluate those at the end of the year. Bonuses and salary adjustments are based on their performance. I want to keep the men working as a team. My experience is that communication is still the biggest barrier to working together. The more effort you put into communicating what's happening and why it's happening, the happier the people are. People don't like to be on the outside. They want to know what's going on, why it's happening. One of my major jobs is to keep the communication open.

KJR: How many employees do you have?

TW: We have thirteen employees at the ranch.

KJR: What do you see for the future of ranching as we go into this new millennium?

TW: Let me circle back and talk a little bit more about the production system because I think that's where it is. As an industry, we're beginning to realize that we are in the *food* business. So how do we take this old heritage — our ranching heritage — and move it toward a consumer product orientation? It's fun to be a cowboy and enjoy the heritage, the way of life, but how do you make a living at it, and how do you provide the product that people want. So many of us are not fully literate in the consumer end of our product. There has to be a more efficient system of production than the old commodity system that we're operating with right now. Currently it's a cannibalistic system. The packer is going to buy these cattle as cheap as he can and buy them on the average in the commodity system. That's no good. What's the incentive for the producer back down the line to produce a higher quality product? There's none. The feed lot is in the feed business. They don't care how efficient your calf is, because they're selling feed to you. The wrong signals are passed back down the system again. The stocker man doesn't care much about the quality of the calves, although he's beginning to because health is such an issue. Basically, he's going to buy them cheap. He's a margin operator, and wants the cattle to grow and move them on to make his margin. The poor guy at the beginning, the producer, is getting mixed signals. At best the signals are negative but most are wrong. The only way the producer, who makes the genetic decisions, can make the right genetic decisions for the best end product, is to have the right signals sent back down through the system to him. The signals in our industry have been terrible. So how do we correct this system? More producers, commercial cow/calf operations, seed stock operations, are asking how to align ourselves to get the right signals and produce the right product. Cattle producers want to get feedback to do the right thing. The producer drives the genetics, buys the bulls, puts the bulls with the cows, and that's where the product starts. If you make mistakes right there, there's no way to correct them.

KJR: As the producer, you're also the one that the consumer knows the least about. Do you think if the consumer understood who you are, the efforts and technology that you've put into your decisions, perhaps you could change their perception?

TW: Yes. That perception will start to change when the consumer recognizes that all our efforts are for their benefit. An example is the concept of source verification, which means that we can take a piece of carcass or meat, at any point, and track it all the way back to the producer. We can find the guy that bred the cow and bull to produce the calf.

KJR: There's a record to track that information?

TW: Yes, there's a record that follows the calf all the way to the end product. So that way, information can flow both ways. If you come back to me and say, "Well, I understand that you raised that calf?" "Yes, ma'am, I did." "What did you do to that calf?" I can pull it up on my computer and show you everything that was done to that calf from the day he was born, even before he was born. The consumer recognizes this to be a better product because I know everything about this calf — I know what it was fed, the vaccines given, the breeding components. I believe consumers will eventually become aware of our efforts and demand to know more about their product and it's producer. When you make information available, first it becomes accepted and then expected — why isn't everybody doing that? To compete in the protein business with pork, poultry and fish — we have to raise the consumer and industry awareness of our product. Once the consumer expresses demand for more information and thus our product, then there is an opportunity to increase margins — make more money and bring more money back to the ranch.

KJR: What do you see as the legacy for Broseco Ranch?

TW: Genetics, employee management, grazing management, are all of equal importance. I think if you were to ask Phil English, who is president of the company, or myself, we have a desire to see the operation be a leader in the industry. We'd like to be at the front doing things that are going to help us in the industry. We have to make money. That's the bottom line in a business. Often the leaders are the ones that are making the most money, and so we want to be a leader. We want to be on the cutting edge. That's the legacy that we'd like to leave, that Broseco is out there trying to do it right.

R.A. Brown Ranch

Interview with Rob Brown and his youngest son, Donnell, at the ranch headquarters in Throckmorton, Texas, on May 25, 1998. The R.A. Brown Ranch has been a family business since 1895. Rob and Peggy Brown have included in the ranch operation all four Brown offspring and their spouses. The family raises registered and commercial cattle as well as Quarter Horses. In 1997 the family ranch was honored with two prestigious awards: "Cattle Business of the Century Award" by the National Cattlemens Beef Association and "Best Remuda Award" by the American Quarter Horse Association.

KJR: How have you structured your family business?

RB: As each child got out of college, we gave them an opportunity to get involved in the family ranch. We developed business partnerships with each child where they had to come up with their own capital or borrow it themselves. Each partnership has started small then has grown and expanded as the children build more credit and borrowing ability. Through these partnerships, we've diversified and vertically integrated in an effort to make our family business big enough and secure enough to support five families.

RB: In preparation for the future, we have created a family limited partnership. This estate-planning tool has allowed us to pass on our inheritance-worth of land and cattle on to the

kids now and save them a great deal of inheritance tax down the road. In the limited partnership I'm the general partner — I still call the final shots. I think I have children that are brighter than I am. Therefore, we're going to work this ranch as a partnership and get everybody's input and make decisions together and do what we think is best for the whole.

KJR: How would you define your wife Peggy's role in the ranch? How are your daughters and daughters-in-law fitting into the family ranch operation?

RB: Peg took over the bookkeeping duties here at the ranch two or three years after my Dad's death in the late '60s. She kept all the books, and registered all the cattle. When Betsy, our oldest daughter, came back from school she took on part of the duties. Today it's all computerized and now with our increase in size and diversity, Peg, Betsy and Kelli, Donnell's wife, run the office. Marianne and Rob A's wife, Talley, have made decisions to be full-time moms without outside work, but they both help us quite often as well.

KJR: What breeds of cattle did you start out raising?

RB: Well, I actually grew up with straight Hereford cattle, both registered and commercial.

KJR: How many breeds do you have now?

DB: Four straight breeds, three hybrids and a composite: Angus, Red Angus, Simmental, Senepol, Senegus, SimAngus, Simbrah and Hotlander.

KJR: Why so many breeds of cattle?

RB: With our breeding programs we can sit down with our customers and help them develop a planned crossbreeding program. We believe that their cows must fit their environment. Then we can help them select a bull that will help their calves best fit their market and offer excellence in growth, maternal and carcass traits.

KJR: Did you develop this composite breed?

RB: Yes. It is a heat-tolerant composite combining Red Angus, Simmental, Senepol and Brahman. Composite breeding is something that the chicken and the hog people have been doing for a good while and they're tough competition. We felt that if it were most efficient for them, why wouldn't it work in the cattle business?

DB: Dad was the main brain behind us building the Hotlander composite here at the ranch. Most of us were quite skeptical at first, but it has worked and worked extremely well!

KJR: What is a Composite Breed?
DB: Let me explain it this way for you. There's straight breeding (pure-breeding), which is mating one breed of cattle to one breed of cattle, (Hereford to Hereford, Angus to Angus). Then there's crossbreeding. Angus crossed to Hereford creates a black baldy. Here is an easy way to look at it. Straight breeding is like a checking account. Genetically, what you put into it is what you get out. If you put good genetics in you will get good purebred offspring. If you put poor genetics in you will get poor purebred offspring.

A crossbreeding program is like a savings account. The same rule applies, where what you put in is what you get out, genetically. If you put good genetics in you will get a good crossbred offspring plus *interest*. That *interest* is heterosis, or hybrid vigor (terms that mean the same thing and can be used interchangeably. Through crossbreeding, you are able to improve the cattle much quicker than you can through years and years and years of selection in a straight-breeding program. The beauty of a composite is that you get the advantages of crossbreeding. Yet, you manage it like a straight-breeding program because you breed Hotlander back to Hotlander and you don't have to constantly be changing breeds.

KJR: How did you decide which breeds you wanted?
DB: We used breed complementary. We looked at the strengths and weaknesses of all the breeds of cattle in the industry and came up with the four that we felt comple-mented each other the most. Each breed is leading the industry in more than one trait, yet the strengths of each breed are different. Therefore we are able to put the best combination together. Each of them bring their own strengths to the table to produce an ideal beef animal.

RB: We selected, Senepol bred to Red Angus (Senegus), and Simmental bred to Brahman (Simbrah). Then, we crossed those two hybrids (Senegus bred to Simbrah) to come
up with the Hotlander. We've ended up with the best traits of all four breeds. They are
moderate-sized cows that are highly reproductive and efficient. In fact they are more
efficient than any other breed we have. We're getting calves that grade a high percentage
Choice, Yield Grade 1 or 2, plus the beef is tender, and the cattle are still heat tolerant.
We know of no other heat tolerant cattle that are coming up with the performance,
carcass merit and eating quality that we are in the Hotlander cattle that we have been
producing since 1991.

KJR: What's the distinction with these four breeds?
DB: With the Hotlander composite, we have a very high level of heterosis (or high
interest rate return) because each of the four breeds is very different. The more different
the breeds there are, the more heterosis you are able to get. Plus they are able to retain
the high level of heterosis year after year. The rule is, the more breeds you have in a
composite population, the more of that *interest*, or heterosis, you are able to keep
throughout the successive generations. Also, contrary to "coffee-shop cowboy talk", the
more breeds you have in the composite, the more uniform the cattle are.

KJR: Why did you feel this composite breed was needed?
RB: We think there's more potential for expansion in the cattle business in the hot,
humid regions of the world so we developed Hotlander to fit that environment. Domestically we are talking east of Interstate 35 and south of Interstate 40, while internationally
we are talking South America, Australia, Asia, and several undeveloped countries. In
these regions, we must have heat-tolerant cattle to be efficient. These cattle could be the
answer for people who need heat-tolerant cattle, but need them to fit the meat quality
specifications of our beef packers. The packers have told us they want no more than 1/4

Brahman and Hotlander fits both that plus the tough environments. The Hotlander cattle are doing so many things right that we believe their future is unlimited.

KJR: Don't you have two sales a year?
DB: We hold a female sale each spring and a bull sale the second Wednesday in October. Our first bull sale was in 1975 where we sold 100 bulls. In 1998 we sold 450 bulls and 650 females.

RB: Since 1970 we have plan-mated each of our one-thousand registered cows individually so that each one can be bred by AI (Artificial Insemination). We take the best bull in the breed, one that best complements the traits of the cow. The objective is to produce the most ideal calf possible from each cow. For example, to produce medium frame-size cattle, we breed larger cows to smaller bulls and smaller cows to larger bulls.

RB: Since Donnell came back to the ranch in 1993 with his computer skills and training in animal breeding and genetics, we have advanced our breeding program to a whole new level. Genetic predictors, called EPD's (Expected Progeny Differences), are the statistical numbers used to identify the genetics of each animal for birth weight, growth traits, maternal traits and carcass traits. Donnell uses a computer spreadsheet to evaluate these genetic predictors to produce the ideal mating where each calf best fits our targets for each of the 15 different traits in which we have EPD's. This helps us find the best 5 bulls in the breed that best fit each cow genetically. Then we go and look at each cow to make the final selection of which one of those 5 bulls best fits each cow and complements her looks.

KJR: You take this information and go out and look at the cattle? Isn't that a combination of instinct and knowledge?
RB: Right. I used to go out and look at the cows using the old head computer but this new way is much more accurate, especially since we now have a lot more information to evaluate.

KJR: Is the farming operation for your own usage, or do you sell product as well?

RB: We farm around 5,000 acres of wheat now. We graze it for 100 days through the winter then combine it in the spring as a cash crop. We also harvest some of it for wheat silage to feed our cows.

KJR: Is the ranch self-sustaining?

RB: Yes, but it hasn't always been profitable. There are good years and bad years.

DB: But it's continued to sustain.

RB: The ranch is a growth stock. We've lived off of it and plowed back into it what we have made to lease more land and buy more cattle.

KJR: What about your Quarter Horse operation?

RB: My father had what he called Quarter Horses. He was one of the men that helped organize the American Quarter Horse Association in 1940. He used to have as many as 80 brood mares at a time. We now have about 35 brood mares. We still pasture breed everything so it's a low-overhead operation where the mares pay their own way. We'll keep three to five colts to break and use for ranch work and then we may keep a replacement filly or two. We normally sell about 20 weanlings at the bull sale each fall when they are just five or six months old. We've always tried to breed a great athlete that had a lot of cow sense and a good mind and good disposition. We have specialized in what we call ranch horses. It's definitely become a specialty, and very popular.

DB: Horse breeding is very frustrating to me because more horses are sold on promotion and propaganda than their true genetic value. With cattle we use EPD's to measure and identify the very best cattle in the world and then mass multiply them with AI and embryo transfer. By doing this we have made huge improvements in cattle. Horse breeders could do that too if they wanted. All of these same tools are right at their fingertips.

RB: I'm still trying to get the Quarter Horse Association to use this same technology and hopefully someday they will.

KJR: How are you preparing for the new millennium?
RB: We feel that as a seedstock breeder, we have to be five or ten years out in front of the rest of the industry to breed what we think the future is going to need. You can't live in the past and build a future. We want to stay on the cutting edge to raise the best cattle we can to help our customers maximize profits.

RB: We have formed an alliance called Rancher's Renaissance with several other major ranches in the United States to decrease risk and improve profits for us as well as our customers. By putting together a group of people that can guarantee that each steak sold is going to be tender, tasteful and healthy we are paid premiums. So we are going to do everything we can from a genetic standpoint to help our customers produce cattle that fit their customer's demands. Then through this alliance, help them get paid the premiums they deserve.

KJR: Donnell, you're the youngest family member, where do you see cattle industry going?
DB: I see us becoming more service-oriented toward our customers. We will take our cattle all the way from conception to consumption. The beef industry is divided into so many different segments: commercial cow/calf production, seedstock production, stockers, feeders, packers, purveyors, and retailers. I see us working together to vertically integrate these segments to capture and share profits through each of them.

KJR: Isn't what you are describing a more holistic approach?
RB: Yes, we want to sell to the end user, the consumer.

DB: Today, everything is sold on the average. In the future I see true value-based marketing where the cattle with superior genetics bring the highest price, and below average cattle will be discounted to the point where they're not profitable to produce. I foresee fewer but larger producers, though probably not the degree of vertical integration we see in the pork and poultry industry because of the land mass and capital investment required to produce cattle.

KJR: What do you think we need to do to increase beef consumption?
DB: I think we in the cattle business have been too hard-headed and have tried to convince the consumer that what we produce is what they need, instead of trying to find out what the consumer wants and produce that.

RB: We need to get our product to where they can go buy it, pop it in the microwave and in ten minutes put something on the table that is delicious, quick, easy and nutritious.

KJR: What legacy do you want to leave?
RB: We want to start with the fact that we left the ranch in better condition, from an ecological standpoint, than we got it. The rancher is a grass farmer, and if he doesn't have grass, he's out of the cattle business. We've learned there's a way to work together in nature, improve our conditions and ensure that it's good for the following generations. That's what makes this ranch continue as a very functional business.

DB: I think there are a couple of legacies that I'd like to leave. One is our family mission statement: We are continuously striving to improve the efficiency of converting God's forage (that which you and I can't eat) into healthy, nutritious and great-tasting beef to better feed His people. The other legacy is that of a God-fearing, God-respecting family that produces some of the most efficient and great-tasting beef cattle in the entire world.

CF Ranch

Interview with Al and Mike Micallef at the CF Ranch headquarters ranch in Alpine, Texas on May 22, 1998. The Micallefs have five ranches and a farm operation in Texas totaling over 125,000 acres plus a ranch in New Mexico. Their multiple businesses include manufacturing and the Reata restaurants.

KJR: What is your philosophy for expanding your ranching business?

AM: In my experience, as in other businesses, ranching appears to be a business that's incremental — the larger you can afford to get, the more efficient you can be. Once you have built the basic infrastructure of a ranching operation, it remains about the same size regardless of how large or small the ranch gets. You can add ranches and add productivity off those ranches for relatively low cost. For example, a ranching operation has large equipment that's needed to manage the operation: bulldozers, back hoes, blades to keep it maintained. If you have a small ranching operation that equipment sits there a good part of the year. If you have a bigger operation, it is used more frequently, but it doesn't cost any more, other than operating it. Another example, once you have an office staff in place — accountant, management — with your management philosophy in place, you can operate five or six or seven ranches, as well as you can operate one or two. You can add an extra 50,000 acres, or you can add an extra four or five hundred head of cattle by adding another cowboy, another pickup truck, and a few incremental pieces of equipment. That can become very efficient. We've tried to be involved in every segment of the ranching operation as well as other income streams. We have a cow/calf operation and a registered operation. We buy bulls from the outside, use a lot of our own bulls and sell bulls. We raise our own replacement cattle. We have stocker cattle and a yearling operation. We have a farm that supplies a limited quantity of hay that we need for our operation. It also affords us the opportunity to buy steers, lightweight steers, and run them on the farm. We retain ownership of our cattle through the feedlot. We are investigating the purchase of, or an interest in, a feed lot. We're trying to be progressive enough to take profit from all segments of the business, from the cow/calf operation to the feed lot operation.

KJR: What factors make this ranch successful?
MM: Retained ownership.

AM: We don't make a move without weighing the risks and knowing where we are economically all the time. That includes figuring the break-even point on each phase before we undertake it.

MM: The management structure is my father and myself, we're the overall management. We give each ranch manager direction, and then give them a lot of latitude to make their own decisions. We have weekly reports on how much they're feeding and what is the body condition score of the cattle. We believe if we can't get cattle bred in 90 days, we might as well not be in the cow business. If you can't get a good breed up and you can't get it in 90 days to be consistent enough, it makes it a lot harder to go onto wheat, and retain your cattle. You want to sell a pen of cattle that are consistent. We've given the cowboys the management on their ranches. They code the bills monthly. All the data is put into the Peachtree Accounting Program. We have our monthly meetings where everyone gets together, which is an important time. It allows us to get personal with each cowboy. We talk about what decisions we need to be making and what we're thinking of doing. We set the parameters and let them run with it. Ranching comes down to being a very low cost producer — the pounds of beef produced and how much it costs you to produce those pounds.

AM: To summarize what Mike is saying, we have taken fellows who have been range cowboys and made them managers of their operations. We've given them the tools and the education — educating them on the outside and on the inside to manage a ranching operation efficiently. If they were to leave us, buy their own ranch or go to a new ranching operation, they would be able to establish it, measure its performance on a monthly basis, and do what is necessary to make it a profitable operation. What we've done is taken a group of cowboys and turn them into managers and ranchers as opposed to just cowboys.

KJR: How much does outside income figure into your ranching operation?
MM: We've been successful at having our ranching operations support themselves and turn a profit. I don't believe, however, that in today's environment and in this part of the country a ranch could pay for its purchase from the funds it produces. In my studies and conversations about how the ranching industry was established in this country, the majority of the ranches were bought with outside income.

KJR: What is the peculiar to this specific environment?
MM: A peculiarity about this country is that our rain doesn't come from storm fronts. Our rain comes in summertime from afternoon buildups, so it's inconsistent. One ranch might get a good rain and a ranch only ten miles away might get half as much rain because that's how the weather pattern builds up with afternoon thunderstorms. The inconsistency in rainfall is our biggest challenge because it's hard to make long term goals.

KJR: What innovations have you introduced?
MM: This industry has always played pretty close to the vest. The first thing that we did was to make everybody that worked for us a part of the operation. We gave them as much understanding about the operation as we possibly could. We have mission statements and critical success factors that we work toward.

AM: We are building cattle and building calves that are going to fit the needs of the industry. We believe that Hereford or English cross cattle are the size that the industry wants. These cattle have the greatest chance of grading in the areas that the packer wants. The diabolical part of this industry is that it pays on the average and doesn't pay any more for quality and consistency. At some point the industry is going to pay for cattle that fit the box the way they should. Some things we are doing in breed selection are a preparation for the future, using genetics to build cattle that the future will be looking for.

AM: We are believers in asset utilization. We measure each one of our properties and determine, based on our management philosophy and mission statement, what we can do with our ranching operations besides eating the grass and drinking the water. For example, we've shot five feature films on our ranches, which has added substantial income to the ranching operations. We have done a variety of television commercials. We occasionally take particular groups onto our ranch that fit our mission statement. We have opened several Reata restaurants that were initially conceived to utilize beef. The restaurants got so successful that we were not able to supply the beef, yet they have added substantial income to our operations overall.

KJR: Are the restaurants under the management of CF Ranches?
AM: They were initially, they are not any longer, because they're big cumbersome operations to manage. The ranches led us into that. We still sell beef into those operations at a premium for the ranching operations.

KJR: Mike, would you read us the ranch mission statement?

MM: It is the mission of CF Ranch Land & Cattle Company to be a profitable entity that is recognized by our competitors, suppliers and customers as being a well-managed, high quality organization. The philosophy is that CF Ranch Land & Cattle Company pledges to provide a working environment that enhances a positive attitude and strong sense of pride in its employees. It is the intention of CF Ranch Land & Cattle Company to create an infrastructure that will support all ranch operations while maintaining a favorable relationship with all other JMK entities and Reata Restaurants. CF Ranch Land & Cattle Company will endeavor to promote these and other JMK and Reata Restaurants to its guests, suppliers and other business contacts. The following are the goals of the CF Ranch Land & Cattle Company: 1) To be a low cost, efficient producer without sacrificing the quality or integrity of the operation; 2) to maximize human resources; 3) to maximize ranch resources without defacing land or overusing the land resources; 4) to produce the product that is selling at maximum value in the market and maintaining an appropriate return on all input; 5) to maximize utilization on all available ranch resources available to us to the greatest degree, whether it be running cattle, entertaining guests or hunting; 6) to remain a leader in maintaining the heritage and resources of West Texas; 7) to develope an environment which is conducive to promoting JMK and Reata Restaurants. What we would like is a 20% return on revenue, 5% to 8% return on assets and absolutely no money being borrowed to run the operations. A budget and plan will be set each year. Annual profit sharing is our bonus program we have with the cowboys.

MM: The criteria for our profit sharing with the cowboys is: 30% of it is based on ranch profit, 20% on conditions and assets under their care, 10% is attitude, 10% loyalty, 10% timely report, 10% team play and 10% understanding the business.

AM: Each winter the maximum possible bonus is figured for each employee, then docks are taken for deficiencies in performance. People really pay attention when you take

money away. We come very close to paying full bonuses because we've got a team of guys that pay attention.

KJR: How are you preparing for the millennium?
AM: I think Mike said the key word is being flexible.

MM: We have to get everything more even, because we've got to produce a quality product and a consistent product for the consumer. Along with cloning is genetic engineering, I think we're trying to build cattle that will prepare us for the next millennium. What we need to do is keep increasing the quality and consistently.

AM: I think gathering more statistical data for more matrix managing.

MM: Are the extra dollars you are adding to gain those extra pounds worth what you are giving up?

AM: On the surface, the ranching operation, business, seems to be simple. But compared to all the business that I've been in, and that is a lot, it is extremely complicated.

KJR: What legacy do you want to leave for future generations?
AM: The legacy I want, as Mike said, is to leave the land in better condition than when we came. I just want our ranching operation to be viewed at the end of our cycle and not at the beginning. If you question everything that's done in the past and try to do things differently, you're ridiculed sometimes. I want to be viewed as being a progressive, good operator.

MM: I want to be the most successful person, successful rancher.

KJR: How would you define that?
MM: It would be, in the end, who is getting more profit off that operation. My definition would be per animal unit, or per head, who's putting the most dollars in his pocket.

AM: For the long term. In the short term anybody can maximize profitability of an operation.

KJR: What do you see for the future of the ranching industry?

AM: I see in the next twenty years, changes that we won't even comprehend, absolutely incredible changes. I think small ranches will be driven out of the business because their costs for operating are going up dramatically and the profitability is going down. A cowboy doesn't just come to work, get married, live on a ranch, die on a ranch and get buried on the ranch anymore. Now they need health insurance, retirement programs and they have to deal with all government agencies, including Workmen's Comp. We have the EPA out here telling us what to do. With all our businesses we come from an environment where we deal with these details every day, so we can integrate them into our ranching operations and make it work for us. But the average small rancher cannot afford the administrative work — it's mind boggling. You could tie up a single employee for whole year filling out paperwork. Small ranchers are not going to be able to do it.

MM: I think we're in big trouble if we don't retain market share. There will always be a percentage of people that have cattle where it really doesn't matter to them how much it costs because they do it as a hobby. But, if you look at the other two meats, no one raises pigs or chicken for a hobby. The raising of pigs and chicken is almost all in hot houses, all indoors.

AM: I believe our industry, has done a terrible job in marketing. We are the victims of very bad information, yet we haven't worked aggressively to change that perception. What hampers this industry is the misconception of a health issue for beef. Consumers are uneducated about beef and it is ruining our market share. Scientific studies have refuted most all the misinformation, yet the industry has not capitalized on these facts. Also, at the top of the industry organizations, politics are making decisions and spending our money inefficiently and ineffectively.

KJR: As father and son, how do you two see ranching differently?

AM: I think, with our overall philosophy, we're both on the same page. Our personalities are different. I try to think differently when I approach a problem or approach an opportunity. Mike gathers a lot of data, makes his decisions based on how other people do things and I think our combination works very well.

MM: I think the biggest difference is personality. That relates to how we do things. I'm more conservative; he's more aggressive and goes out there and gets things done. I'd rather move into something slowly to make sure we don't over use a resource. Make sure that we're on safe footing.

AM: We've come from two different generations. Mike's job in life is preserving and growing. My job was finding it and making it. He has a different role and I'm glad. I'm glad he's that way. He's taught me a lot in the last couple of years, because he has a more formal education connected with the ranching industry than I do.

MM: At 23, I don't think, Dad, you were as scared to death of lawsuits. At this age, I'm scared of the lawsuits and EPA and everybody else. You've got this huge government that's looming over you. Yet over the years, the government hasn't managed anything better. The people who are going to manage the land best are the people that have to make a living from it. For example, government for years has managed wildlife and we nearly used it up. Then Texas, more than any other state, put a dollar price on wildlife. Now we have higher game numbers on white-tailed deer, more than we ever had. When you put a dollar figure on something then it has value to people and they'll preserve it and manage it.

AM: Also, there are certain things that we won't do, for example, we won't mine. We won't deface or scar the land — we will not do anything that could scar the earth permanently. That's our philosophy.

6666's Ranch

Interview with J.J. Gibson and his son Mike and daughter-in-law Shonda at the headquarters ranch in Guthrie, Texas, on July 23, 1998. The Four Sixes, 6666, is one of the historic Texas ranches founded in 1900 by Samuel Burk Burnett. When he died it passed to his granddaughter, Anne Burnett Tandy in 1922. After her death in 1980 ownership passed to her daughter Anne. W. Marion and granddaughter Windi Phillips.

KJR: When did you start working for the ranch?

JJG: Our relationship with the 6666 started when my father was living here at the time Burk Burnett bought the ranch in 1900. My father had his own place. He had homesteaded a place, but it was unfenced and his cattle ran with the Burnett cattle until such time they fenced it, about 1920. I started working for them in 1946 when I got out of the Marines after World War II and worked here until 1948. I wanted to get married and left because I got a better job. We were gone until a management position became open in 1969 or 1970. This has been Mike's home since he was ten years old.

KJR: How has the ranch grown over the years?

JJG: In the early days this rolling plains of Texas was a breeding area, they would send their cattle north. They didn't merchandise them until they were three and four year olds. As time progressed they improved the genetics and now we sell the cattle as yearlings.

Today our yearlings grow as big as the former three and four year old cattle — all because of improved genetics.

MG: We buy outside bulls to keep our bloodlines fresh. But our Hereford herd, it's uninterrupted.

JJG: It's always been straight Hereford and horned Hereford. Hopefully, it always will be. But, we recognized back in the late 1960's that for some of our environment, we needed cross-bred cattle. We started cross-breeding. Now we're cross-breeding with Angus bulls on the Hereford cows, one time, and then we keep that black baldy female. Then we breed her back to an Angus bull. Since we feed our own cattle, we found that that carcass is more acceptable. We're going to pursue that vigorously.

KJR: Why did you feel you needed to bring in an outside influence?
MG: The eastern part of this ranch is really rough and has a lot of cedar and rock. The relief and the topography are tough.

JJG: The one great factor that influenced our decision was the cedar and now the cedar fly. The Hereford didn't handle it well. The cedar fly is worse now than it was twenty years ago — they have spread. We needed tougher cross-bred cattle to get up into that range.

MG: They can utilize the country and it's a long way between water holes.

JJG: They handle the heat a little bit better. They are a little more durable.

MG: They'll raise a real good calf down in that country, where Herefords will just raise a little ball of hair, because she just can't get out and graze in the heat or tolerate the cedar flies.

JJG: The cedar flies will not let them graze. The flies keep bothering them and that white Hereford brisket will be bleeding, blood running down their flanks.

MG: They bother the black cattle, but the blacks seem to tolerate them and handle it better.

JJG: Since we feed our own cattle, we've learned some things and we have first-hand information. We are trying to raise an animal with a carcass that's going to be acceptable in the 21st century, and that's just around the corner. We think we're on the right road.

JJG: One of these days these big feed lot operators are going to own these cattle all the way to the grocery store, through the packer. I can see some of it starting today and if you're going to be in the ball game, you're going to have to have the right kind of cattle that's going to be acceptable to them.

KJR: Do you think that more producers will start feeding their own cattle?
JJG: I think there's a possibility that some will, although, people were burnt this last year doing that.

MG: There's a lot of risk. You risk an awful lot by feeding your own cattle. You're financially exposed a lot more than just selling them as calves or backgrounding them and selling them as yearlings. Over the years it's been profitable for us. The last two years haven't been good and this year is the worst year we've had.

KJR: Is that because of the drought and lack of grass?
JJG: No, it's the cattle prices. I can't explain to you this terrific drop in prices.

MG: They keep saying it's numbers, number of cattle on the market, but the numbers don't add up. We should be coming out of this low cycle. We should have been headed out of it already. Everybody else had anticipated that we would be and that's the reason they bought cattle high and now, they're taking big losses in the feed lot.

KJR: Do you see ranches getting bigger?

JJG: I think we'll have some corporate ranches where people maybe have outside income. I also think there will also be some smaller producers that do a lot of their own work and maybe have an heir to their land — there will still be that type of rancher.

MG: You know, this is not a business you get rich in anyway. Corporate ranches, sure, we're going to have some of them. They're not going to be wildly successful, I don't think. The profit margin is too small. When they look at the stock market they can get 20% on that money somewhere else.

JJG: It's very sad. They can take the money out of these ranches and put it in the stock market and return more for the dollar.

KJR: How does outside income influence the 6666?

JJG: The ranch runs itself. It's made with the cattle and the horses. Mike makes up a budget and each ranch makes up a budget. Shonda has her input into it, the things that she needs to run this headquarter's ranch household, and we submit that budget once a year to Mrs. Anne Marion and she approves it. We don't ask for anything.

KJR: How many ranches are there?

JJG: There's just two now but we have had more. I have a personal ranch that my other son is involved with.

KJR: Shonda, how long have you and Mike been married and what do you do here?

SG: We've been married ten years, seven years in this house. I see to the maintenance of the house, the grounds and then I do the office work. Each employee is responsible for their own yard, but I oversee the maintenance, such as when water heaters or air conditioners go out, repairs and things of that nature. This ranch house is not your average little house — it has 11 bedrooms, 14 bathrooms, landscaping — lots of domestic engineering.

SG: Living here in Guthrie becomes challenging handling details when you're 90 miles from shopping and supplies. Twice a week we try to get groceries, fresh flowers and produce.

KJR: How many cowboys do you have working?
MG: I have five camp men — there are five line camps on this ranch. In other words, there's a house, a barn, on five different areas and those gentlemen live there. They are responsible for the camps and a lot of country. They are there to check the water, check the fences, and look after the cattle. They all have families — I don't have any single men here. There are other people — I have a shop man, a windmiller. I have two guys who do nothing but brush work, so I have other personnel. It's just that there's ten cowboys. We operate a store and we have lots of employees, doing other things besides just cowboying. Across the highway we do breed a few mares.

KJR: Would you describe your horse program?
MG: Doctor Blodgett runs the horse program. We have quarter horses and performance quarter horses and stand some running thoroughbreds. I imagine we're breeding around 75 ranch mares this year, and then I'm sure we've bred over 750 mares this year. These are horses that we own, some of them we partnership own, some of them we just stand here. It's a diverse group. We're going to have a horse sale this fall, October 3rd. It will be the first time we've had a sale since 1980. Most of the time we market our fillies without having a sale and the geldings we've generally just raised and used on the ranch.

JJG: It's hard to have a sale every year.

MG: We've pulled a wagon out twice a year for six or seven weeks and we use up a lot of horses real quick. Working in the summer, we use up a lot of horses. "Pulled a wagon out" is an old expression — we used to take the wagon out and set it up, now we camp it right here at headquarters. We feed at the wagon when we come in from working and we can change our horses. We may be working down on this end of the ranch in the morning and up here in the afternoon. Our mobility allows us to get a lot more done.

JJG: Before Mike's time, I'd move the wagon around. There are times that we'd get weathered in someplace — it did rain back in those days — and we'd get rained in and we were just tied up. We couldn't do anything. That's not the case here. The way Mike runs it now, he puts the wagon up here at headquarters and if it rains down there, he's on the phone or radio and knows it. He can change his plan and go some other place.

MG: Also, the wagon helps with Doc Blogett's box lunches, down at the race barn. It's a big help to him when he's breeding in the spring. He has nearly as many people working down there as I have working here.

KJR: During a busy day, how many cowboys would you be feeding?
MG: About 40. Half of them are part-time help.

JJG: One thing I'd like to say about these horses, it's really a help to Mike to have the quality of horses we have here at the ranch. It helps him keep quality cowboys because when cowboys get on here, they don't leave. Cowboys love their horses and they just don't want to leave them. He has a lot better quality people by having these good quality horses.

MG: Each cowboy has about eight head of horses and that depends on if they've got kids — how many little kids they've got. It's important. That's something else that keeps the men happy is if their kids can go with them. Even if they don't come back to work here,

we're teaching the kids something that's going to help them down the line. A lot of kids are not learning the work ethic anymore. We teach them to work

JJG: There are two major problems here, in dealing with management — drought and brush. I've been laying pipelines for water on this ranch since 1971 and Lord, I don't know how many miles of pipeline are here now. Of course, you've always got cattle prices, but that's something you don't have any control over and you don't control the drought either. The only one you can control is the brush if you have enough money.

KJR: What do you think you've done with innovations?
JJG: I think we were one of the pioneers in cross-breeding and we were one of the first to start feeding our own cattle, if you want to call that an innovation.

KJR: How are you preparing for the millennium?
JJG: We've got to survive this one first. As I told you a while ago, I think it's having the right kinds of animals to merchandise. I think that's going to be the key to getting along in the new century. Beef has lost a lot of market share to pork and chicken and other competitive foods. We have to recapture part of that market that we've lost. We're going to have to have cattle and produce the right kind of carcass to sell, and hopefully get a premium for it instead of a discount.

MG: I went to Texas Tech and I got a degree in agriculture. I probably should have gotten a degree in business.

KJR: How has ranching changed from your dad's generation?
MG: We have to watch every little thing very closely. It used to be that you'd pretty much run a ranch out of your day book in your shirt pocket. Not now.

JJG: Shonda has everything on the computer now.

MG: You lose so much before you ever get to your bottom line now. I mean insurance and workmen's comp, everything is so much higher than it used to be. Lots of things that you never even worried about.

JJG: You owe so much when you start the beginning of the year.

MG: Pickups cost $30,000. We're still getting 59 cents for the fat cow. My joke with my neighbor is that I've already started practicing, "you want cheese, and a large coke with that, sir?"

KJR: Shonda, you and Mike are working as partners. Is this different from how you were raised?
SG: Somewhat. I grew up mainly in farming, but it's still agriculture. If you can survive the downs, your ups are pretty good.

MG: Another threat to ranching it that the recreational use of this land is becoming a higher value than raising cattle. It's not here. It won't ever be here. It's too damn harsh an environment. We don't have any water. It's too hot in the summer and too cold in the winter. But other places, people are going to quit running cattle on that land and use it for recreation of some kind.

KJR: What would you like your contribution to be, your legacy?
MG: We're just trying to survive right now, try to get through this cycle. Next spring, it will be better. If I can live long enough and we can stay in business long enough, I'm going to kill all this damned brush, some way or another. That will be my legacy.

JJG: I would like my legacy to be my good judgement of horses and cattle and to be respected by my peers in the cattle industry. Most of all I want to be remembered as a good cowman.

J.D. Hudgins, Inc.

Interview with Bob Hudgins at the ranch headquarters in Hungerford, Texas, on May 28, 1998. The J.D. Hudgins ranch operation was started in 1915 by J.D. and son, Walter Hudgins. The operation has remained in the family and is divided into five divisions: Hudgins, Locke, Forgason, Koonce and Mangum, all family members.

KJR: When did the first Hudgins arrive in Texas?
BH: Joel Hudgins first came to Texas from Virginia in 1839. His son J.D. Hudgins, whom the ranch is named after, was the one first involved with the humped cattle. Back then, they weren't known as Brahman. The first of the humped cattle arrived in the US about 1906.

KJR: At that time were they preferable over the Longhorn?
BH: Yes, they were a little beefier cattle. Although at that time these cattle weren't bred for beef, they had originated from India as work cattle. They were not recognized for beef until the breed association got together and started competing with other cattle breeds. Some early ranchers bought bulls and put them with their native cattle because they were so adaptable to our hot and humid climate. The first rule of adaptation is, can it survive? In fact today, from Florida to almost Arizona, you need a touch of Brahman in most commercial herds to exist. Brahman cattle not only adapt; they thrive in these climates.

However, we do have a barrier going north due to the cold weather because they're short-hair cattle

KJR: You're shipping some bulls today, to Nicaragua? You market internationally?
BH: Yes. It's a year-in, year-out business; at least 50% of our cattle are sold internationally. It's a big market for us. We sell mainly to the Latin countries and Mexico — since Mexico is our neighbor, it is easy to transport these cattle there. Otherwise we truck our cattle from here to Miami then they are flown to South America. You would think Houston would be the port to export from but it costs more to fly from Houston. These cattle today will be shipped out by truck to Miami, put in a quarantine facility for probably 24 hours, or a little less, and then flown to Managua. The flight is four hours to Nicaragua, about five hours to Colombia.

KJR: What is the focus of your domestic market?
BH: The domestic market buys our commercial type bulls, which go into F-1 breeding programs. That is cross-breeding Brahman bulls with Hereford, or Angus, or other breed cows to produce a hybrid cross. That crossbred female is the most popular female in this area and along the gulf coast. Our commercial type bulls mainly stay in the US. We do sell a few commercial foreign, but not that many. Our international sales are registered American Brahman with an estimated 80% of our females being exported.

KJR: Do your international customers buy bulls and semen?
BH: They do both. They buy bulls and inseminate depending on what countries have good insemination programs. So we do sell semen internationally. We don't sell it domestically. It gets to the point that you don't know how much harm you're doing sending that semen overseas, because we'd really like them to buy bulls. Although, sending semen does open up another means of income. You know if a buyer has a good program for insemination, he's less likely to buy a bull. You have to weigh both factors.

KJR: What are the challenges to conducting international business?

BH: Just like this Nicaraguan shipment, they have the Central American cattle show in July that we'll go to. Also we participate in international seminars, for example, in countries like Colombia. They invite me down there to conduct a seminar before a show and I'll show slides and exchange ideas. They appreciate that. So far this year, family members have gone to Mexico, Colombia, Brazil, Costa Rica, Paraguay and Venezuela. Sometimes, you don't want to go because of the politics, but you still need to. For example, travel in Colombia is a little shaky at this time. They have an economic problem along with the guerilla problem of kidnappings. I like the country. It's a pretty place but you can't go to certain areas. You can go to the shows, but there may be a ranch 20 miles out of the city you can't go to.

KJR: Is it because you're an American?

BH: No, not necessarily — it's everybody. The other day we had a senator from down there visit here whose ranch is about an hour out of Bogota. He will take 40 military people with him when he goes to his ranch. He won't spend the night. That's just a way of life down there and it's very hard on them. It's amazing to them to come up here and see how we live out on the ranch with no problems at all. In spite of these challenges, it is still important for us to go there because they have good cattle and have invested a lot of money in their cattle. But their political situations affect us directly.

KJR: How many family members are involved today?

BH: There are five family divisions: Hudgins, Locke, Forgason, Koonce and Mangum involved in this ranch. That's about 50 family members supported by these Brahman cattle. In our division Hudgins, there are five brothers. I'm the fourth generation. The fifth generation is active now. In 1962, we formed a corporation, J.D. Hudgins, Inc. with five divisions of the Hudgins family. Since then we've maintained the same program for selling and promoting our cattle. The land and cattle are separate and the management is separate. When we get ready to sell or show our cattle we put them all together as J.D. Hudgins, Inc. These cattle are numbered, or branded, where you can identify the different divisions. Some customers can tell by the animal's brand which division it comes from, but in selling our cattle the division brand makes no difference. We try to find the best animals available at the time. You want to satisfy a customer and we depend on repeat customers. We want them to come back and buy more cattle next year.

KJR: Is there competition among the divisions?

BH: You don't want a lot of competition, but sometimes it is good. We do have a little competition when we show the cattle. Only the top cattle from the ranch are shown. Before our show string goes out on the road a selection committee from the ranch inspects the cattle At least one representative from each division is selected. We'll go to the show barn and pick out the best cattle for the show string. Of course, everybody wants their cattle to go out on the road and compete and maybe win. There is some competition among the sale cattle because you'd like your cattle to sell first because that way you have less feed bill, less expense in them. We all try to improve every year. You can't afford to slip because the competition is always there.

KJR: Where is the J.D. Hudgins headquarters?

BH: We're all here in Hungerford. All of our family divisions are based out of this office. We have a corporation meeting once a month. We all sit down at a big long table and bring up everything we need to, old business, new business. We find out what problems we have and how the corporation is running. The best thing to do is lay everything on the table. If you've got a problem, you bring it to the board.

KJR: How does your corporate structure work?

BH: All of our sale cattle are branded on the right hip, half circle L. On all animals that are sold with half circle L on them, we take out a five percent commission on the sales.

That goes back to the corporation for operating expenses. We have one full-time secretary and another one part time. So when a buyer writes a check for a bull it's written to J.D. Hudgins, Inc. The secretary takes five percent out and the rest goes to the owner of that bull. That money also pays for labor at the show facility and at our sale pens. We have a very minimal labor force here. All the cattle work is done by the owners — all hands-on. We trust ourselves to take customers out and everything is a private treaty sale. It's more personable to have an owner take a customer out and show him our cattle. I think they appreciate that.

KJR: What do you think makes the ranch operation successful?
BH: One is that our cattle are honest cattle. In other words when people buy cattle from J.D. Hudgins, Inc., we stand behind them 100%. Another is the reputation of our J.D. Hudgins brand identity. We all work to stay together. There are differences within us as far as ideas, management, down to the selection of the cattle. Sometimes you need really easy hands with certain people and you have to respect those differences.

KJR: How many of the new generation are returning from college to participate in the business?
BH: There's probably two from each division that's come back now, but we also see some leaving.

KJR: How do you work your show facility?
BH: We fit our own cattle. We have a small facility right out of town where we'll bring our best ones to fit them. They are fitted here under our management. We started showing cattle in 1932 and make around five shows a year, Houston and Dallas being the most important shows for us.

KJR: Let's say I want to see a bull, where would you take me?

BH: I'd have to ask you what kind of program do you have? Do you have a registered Brahman program, or do you have a commercial program? We would go to different places depending on your needs. Our commercial bulls are in one area. Our better bulls are scattered around different divisions and our show bulls are at one facility. So I would become acquainted with you, what you're looking for. I may be wasting your time showing a high-priced bull if it didn't fit your program. We'll go right to where we need to look. At the sale facilities, we have 21 different pens with bulls on one side and heifers on the other. It's easy for our customers to select what they want. It's sort of a shopping center. Each pen is priced according to quality, with all animals being of similar size. It's easy for us and easy for our customers.

KJR: What has made your J.D. Hudgins brand so successful, today?

BH: Our past generations. My father, Edgar Hudgins and grandfather, Walter Hudgins stood behind their cattle 100%. They dealt honestly with all of their customers. Those two factors are still our number one priority today. When our international guests visit they feel comfortable. We treat them right. Normally, we would have already visited them in their countries. You would be surprised how many friends we have in other countries. Probably just as many friends internationally as we do domestically. Also, it's a certain type of cattle. It's a beef-type animal with a good disposition. They're cattle with good bone and cattle that adapt to their areas. There's no doubt that the J.D. Hudgins' trademark and the pedigrees in these cattle bring a little more dollar-wise.

KJR: What about the reputation of a bad disposition in Brahman cattle?

BH: In the '50's and early '60's, when we had a lot of labor, we tolerated it. We could get by with a bull that would be active. Now we don't tolerate bad-dispositioned cattle. We're too old to try to climb a fence. Over a period of years, you breed the gentle cattle; you breed bulls with good dispositions; breed females that are easy to handle. Their disposi-

tion evolves from genetics. Also, it's management, and being around those cattle all the time — getting used to people. These cattle are very intelligent, so treat them right and they'll remember that.

KJR: Do you advertise in foreign countries?
BH: I think it's the cattle that do the talking — how they perform in those countries. If the cattle perform well, the customer will come back and buy more. They have very competitive shows internationally. If our cattle compete in those shows and do well, that's a big plus for us.

KJR: Do you do any other farming outside of what you need for your own cattle?
BH: Everything is cattle. We do have some hay plots set aside.

KJR: I have to ask the proper pronunciation, is it Brahman, Brahma or Bramer?
BH: Brahman. Brahman is the word. Brahma is a cowboy term. In Latin America, it's Brahman. That's the word to use when you're promoting your cattle — it's a little more dignified when you say Brahman.

KJR: Do you have any outside income for the ranch?
BH: It's all cattle. This ranch operates 100% on cattle. All the cattle we raise are Brahman, no commercial cattle — it's a 100% registered Brahman.

KJR: What innovations have you made?
BH: We're a pretty low-key bunch. We have to keep breeding better cattle. The show ring sometimes dictates size in all breeds, but realistically, we've brought them back to a moderate-framed animal. Daddy always preached to us back then — moderation is the best and that's exactly right. I think we're just practical people trying to keep on improving our cattle. Most of us have gone to universities and come back home. It's hands-on work and being here all the time.

KJR: How are Brahman cattle suited as beef cattle?

BH: We want to breed beef-type animals within the Brahman breed. We have to maintain the beef quality in these cattle. We have to produce a bull that when used in crossbreeding will produce an animal that performs in the feedlot as well as on the rail. The right kind of Brahman cattle will work. Texas A&M has recent studies that show very positive research results for the breed. A lot of the negative perception is unjustified if you breed the right type of Brahmans. Because we are identifiable — with a hump, loose skin and a little ear we are sometimes criticized. If we didn't have a hump, there's no way they could tell the difference. It is a perception. We're not going to take the hump off these cattle because that's our trademark. A Brahman has a hump. A Hereford has a white face. We're going to maintain the hump as a breed characteristic. In fact, it's something we breed for because in the Latin countries they prefer an animal with a big hump. A big hump that sits up straight suggests purity of blood.

KJR: How about the future as we move into the new millennium?

BH: We have to be able to compete with other domestic beef breeds and also to maintain our international market. We have to keep promoting and breeding the right kind of cattle. Breed your own type of cattle and stand behind them 100% percent. That's what keeps customers coming back.

KJR: What do you see as a legacy for J.D. Hudgins?

BH: I hope that we've contributed to the beef industry, not only domestically but also throughout the world. I think our reputation is being honest and personable with everybody we deal with.

McAllen Ranch

Interview with Jim McAllen and James McAllen Jr. at the ranch headquarters in Linn, Texas, on July 14 and 15, 1998. The McAllen ranch dates back to the Santa Anita land grant by the King of Spain in 1791. It has belonged to the descendants ever since and today is owned by the James McAllen family.

KJR: Is it your immediate family that owns the ranch today?

JMC: Yes, my children and I. There are no other owners. We've bought out all the other cousins that were involved. Today, it's up to us and we work very diligently to carry it on to the next generation which is my son, James' generation. My daughters play an active role in different capacities, one is going to school and the others live with their husbands. James is 21, learning the trade, living the day-to-day life of going through the school of hard knocks. It's not beaches and fine places for a 21-year-old to hang out, but it's a great life and he really enjoys it.

KJR: Do you have outside help beyond the family?

JMC: We used to have about 25 employees. We're down to six employees here at the headquarters. Unlike the old days, it's not economically feasible to have the employees that the ranches deserve nowadays.

KJR: Why is that?

JMC: Our power of selling cattle and our marketing power isn't there anymore. Today there's a reluctance to eat beef and I think it's a pendulum that's gone way too far one way. I think slowly people will realize that they've made a mistake and will start eating red meat again. I think beef will come back, if everybody doesn't go broke between now and that time — it's a real concern. If the American farmer and rancher and agriculturist go broke, where are the American people going to buy their food? This is a very serious concern. We live a life of luxury eating out of our horn of plenty and it's going to dry up one of these days, if we don't take care of our young, up-and-coming people in agriculture. As ranchers, we don't receive any government subsidies. We don't farm the government subsidies. We don't have that luxury. We have to live day by day and tighten our belts when we can. About every ten years we have a good year, but a lot of people can't survive.

KJR: What kind of cattle were on the ranch originally?

JMC: The native cattle were the forefathers of the Longhorn. Looking at the old pictures they weren't all these colorful cattle you see today. Their horns weren't tremendously big. They were long, but most of them were blacks or brindles or reds. They were common cattle, Corriente. During the 1880's my great grandfather brought in some Hereford bulls and started the process of improving the herd on the ranch. I remember as a kid that all the cattle were wild and mean. It would take about two months to gather them on the ranch. Then in 1942, my dad was one of the first to buy Beefmaster cattle and bring them into our herd. Since that time, we've been breeding Beefmaster cattle. We've tried various breeds and found that the Beefmaster cattle have done the best surviving the conditions we have here.

KJR: Would describe your conditions?

JMC: It's entirely different from the rest of the United States because of the weather conditions. It can be very lush or it can be very severe — you're seeing its worst this summer. It can be very, very hot and then it can be very, very cold. Over the long haul in the heat, the pure European cattle breeds cannot survive. We've tried them all.

KJR: Has outside income figured into this operation?

JMC: No. The outside income has not figured into this operation. Although there is oil and gas production on the land, it does not go into the same coffers of the ranching operation. The ranch is self-sustaining and always will be.

KJR: What innovations have you developed?

JMC: One of our innovations is in wildlife management. When I was growing up my father had one of the best managed game ranches in South Texas. His method of game management was abstention. You couldn't hunt anything. So he became the seed stock for the general area of South Texas.

KJR: What game was in this area?

JMC: the wild game was primarily white-tailed deer and javelin. People were just coming out of the depression when he took over the management of the ranch. They had lived off the land and literally head-lighted, trapped, snared, roped on horseback anything they could eat. When my father came along, he started killing beef calves for the help to eat so then their attention was not on the wild game — he put wild game off-limits. I came along in the '50s and became interested in wildlife. In 1968 we bought the Guajolota Ranch and in '77 decided to game proof it and started a wildlife management program. I hired a game biologist and with his expertise and my guidance we immediately started working on the ratios of buck to does. The neighbors had killed all the bucks so we had a ratio of maybe one buck to 12 does. A normal ratio in wildlife is probably one buck to 2.5 does. We systematically began to allow the bucks to grow older and allow those majestic specimens within the ranch to remain as herd sires. We changed the ratio to 1:1. Next we started cultivating custom hunters. My theory was that if sportsmen pay big bucks to hunt an elk in Colorado, they may want to hunt our elusive white-tail deer for the same amount. This redirected the focus of the ranch to wildlife. The ranch booked up the first year.

KJR: Were white tail deer indigenous to this area?

JMC: They were indigenous but they had been hunted out. Once we started managing white-tail deer, we only hunted nine days a year. We only harvested ten percent of the adult males and equal females. I acquired a scientific game breeder's license and began breeding superior bucks to release onto the ranch as herd sires. Today, some of these superior bucks are living legends. I invented and installed wildlife waterers so that water is available year around and is trouble free. Water is more important than feed. These waterers are strictly a haven for the wildlife: deer, quail, turkey and javelin and many migratory birds — the cattle don't use them. The wildlife is free-ranging with the cattle within the ranch's 7,000 acres. The ranch is game-proof.

KJR: What is game proofing?

JMC: Game-proofing is an eight foot fence primarily where the deer cannot cross. The coyotes, bobcats and javelin do get across, but your deer do not. That controls the ingress and egress of the smaller animal. What you don't want is your neighbor's does coming over. Then your ratios are thrown out of proportion. It's not that you don't want your deer out, it's that you don't want your neighbor's deer in. Like other hunting, birding and nature operations around the world the bottom line motivation has made everyone aware of the value of preserving our most precious commodity, our wildlife. It's just like Africa. When there was hunting there was no poaching. You stop the hunters and in come the poachers.

KJR: Did your management of not hunting the biggest buck affect your custom hunting program?

JMC: Absolutely not. In fact, it gives our program more integrity and therefore a little more notoriety. People have seen the results of our management efforts in Texas and now people all over the United States are managing white-tail deer. There is a great reward to see that your management is creating superiority and balance that should have been there normally in nature, which in the wild is the survival of the fittest.

KJR: Would you explain the Valley Land Fund?

JMC: I was on the founding board of an organization known as the Valley Land Fund, which operates in four South Texas counties. This fund buys small tracks of land to preserve its prime brush habitat. The Valley Land Fund organized itself to preserve those lands then came to ranchers like myself and asked if we would like to pay to join a contest. They invited wildlife photographers from all over the world to team up with ranchers and landowners. Every two years the fund sponsors a "high-stakes" wildlife photo contest with a cumulative prize of $100,000. The rancher/landowner and the photographer share the prize money. This contest has helped make ranchers/landowners and the public more aware of their wildlife resources.

KJR: Have you ever won?

JMC: Yes, four years ago, I won $8,000 and two years ago, I won another $8,000. I put all that money back into wildlife preservation — more wildlife waterers, retreats for the birds and made studios for the photographers.

KJR: How do you and the photographer work together?

JMC: I furnish the place, give him the guidance of where I think he can get the best photographs. The Valley Land Fund dues and contest entry fees go into the pot to buy more land, as do the sponsors assigned to the ranchers and the photographer. With the winning photography they produce calendars, T-shirts and coffee table books — there

are two books so far. Prior to the contest, the people of the Rio Grande Valley did not realize the richness of their wildlife. This will be our third contest coming up — a total of six years. It is fabulous. They have a program for school kids to come see these photographs. They have presentations on the television. All of a sudden the people have become more aware of the wildlife and they put more value on native brush land. They see that hunting, cattle and birding all fit together and do work.

KJR: What do you see for the future of ranching?
JMC: On the financial side, there needs to be restrictions on importation of beef. American beef is the safest meat-product ever, anywhere in the world. All you have to do is go to any foreign country, look at their meat counter, see their meat processing, and you can visualize the problems that they might have. Yet, we're importing that beef without the restrictions that are put on us and at the same price. The same applies to all agricultural products: corn, grains or vegetables. We impose stiff requirements on cantaloupes and strawberries, so they are exported to Central America. Then we import the foreign produce a lot cheaper. US agriculture needs to be allowed to be competitive. Don't let my generation be the last one that produces agricultural products. Don't do that.

JMC: As it is, we have enough trouble with inheritance tax to survive. The biggest detriment to wildlife is the death tax. For example, half of my neighbor's place, 2,500 acres, was sold off to pay the inheritance tax. It was divided into five blocks of 500 acres apiece. Then came the mobile home, the kids, the cats, the dogs and each block now has a new electric line to a new water well. The integrity of open land has been destroyed because somebody had to sell 2,500 acres to save 2,500 acres. That is the biggest detriment to wildlife, to ranching, to all agriculture.

KJR: What legacy would you like to leave for future generations?

JMC: Today it's hard to pass the torch to your children and not bind them up so tight that their way of living is not as comfortable. I would like to see this ranch go another two or three generations; just as my father, my grandfather, my great grandfather and the first Spaniard that my family married. You can't be blind to tradition. You must think of the overall family — what's right at the time and respect that. Other members of the family chose not to continue, we chose to continue. I think we're a healthier family by doing that. However, the herd of cattle or wildlife within the ranch should never diminish the quality of the family life. Today we're running the ranch and cattle with very high technology. We're doing DNA analysis on cattle and tenderness tests. This is the wave of the new rancher, the wave of my son. It is the only way that we can compete with other meats that aren't as good, or as flavorful or as healthy as beef. We're learning to feed cattle better; we're learning the genetics that produce cattle with leaner, tastier beef, and it is even better.

KJR: How would you distinguish this part of Texas from the rest of the state?

JMJ: The Rio Grande Valley is really where ranching and cowboy traditions started, in my opinion. These traditions came up from northern Mexico and their Spanish origins. This region was settled over 200 years ago, before the United States or Texas was established.

KJR: Were you raised with Spanish or English as your first language?

JMJ: My ancestors came from Spain. Growing up as a kid I was surrounded by Spanish. We spoke Spanish in the house, with my father, especially with the *vaqueros*. We had to communicate in Spanish when you went into town. It surrounded you all the time: the culture, the food, the way of life, the siestas in the afternoon. When our family gets together, we seem to say or express what we feel better in Spanish. When I hear my cousin speak Spanish I always have a warmer place in my heart. My dad would rather speak Spanish, especially when he meets somebody that's Hispanic, even though they

might know English. He's just not comfortable speaking English to somebody that's of Hispanic origin — he just doesn't think it's right. I've had people tell me that they think my dad prefers to speak Spanish anyway, and I believe it. It's an emotional language and it's fun. I enjoy it.

KJR: Why have the Beefmaster breed of cattle worked for you?

JMJ: We were one of the first Beefmaster breeders, other than the originators. These cattle have done extremely well for us, especially for this region, because they're heat-tolerant and very fertile. They're an ideal cow. Maternally, they're very good mothers, which is important to us. When you get into these extreme conditions like we have now, you depend on her being a good mother. A live calf is how a ranch makes money. If that cow can give her calf everything she's got, that's what we need. In spite of this difficult year they look in great shape because they've been eating mesquite beans. We can't burn the prickly pear because all the cactus has dried up. When you start burning pear with dry cactus it is more fibrous and the cows develop what's called pear ball. That fiber collects in their rumen and keeps balling up and will eventually kill the cow. We've been feeding hay and some other mineral trying to keep some supplement out there. We're trying not to feed too heavily because once you start feeding, you don't stop until it rains and we have no idea when it's going to rain. Feeding is our largest expense and blows away the budget when you look at the income statements.

KJR: You're the next generation and have many choices. You went away to school in the East and now you are back to ranch, why?

JMJ: I'm fifth generation and I've always known what I wanted to do since I was in first grade. I always wanted to be a rancher; always wanted to be a cowboy; although, in my opinion, I'm not actually a cowboy. Times have changed. Today you get a pickup, load your horse in the trailer and take off. My grandfather would leave on horseback on Monday and not return until Friday. He camped out with the rest of the *vaqueros*, gathering, working and herding cattle. He went by wagon to fix windmills and fences. While he was out his wife was doing the books at home making sure everything was handled. Nowadys it seems like a lot of the art has been taken out of what cowboys do. Back then you couldn't run to the store. You had to make your own gear. You had to make your own rawhide and leather plus do your own repairs. Today I can pick up a catalog, order what I need and it will be delivered the next day by ten o'clock. I think the essence of the true cowboy has been lost.

JMJ: Getting back to what I wanted to do — it was always to be a rancher. Being the only boy in the family, there is a lot of pressure on you, that's for sure. I don't resent that because my dad got me so interested in what we're doing out here it is really what I love to do. I wouldn't want to be any other place in the world. This is where I belong; this is my home and I plan to be here for the rest of my life.

KJR: Are you carrying the weight of that fifth generation?
JMJ: It is a pressure, having to live up to my grandfather and my father and their strong ways of work. There's nothing like experience and I'm learning every single day. After being out of school for two years, I think I've learned more in these two years than I have in four years of college. I believe much of the pressure I feel is in my mind. My parents, especially my father, would like me to run the ranch. They've always said I can do whatever I'd like and they truly believe that. I think I'm lucky to know that I want to stay here, my schooling on the East Coast really taught me that. From the eighth grade until twelfth I had a chance to step back and take a look at where I was from — the traditions that I was a part of, the culture that I came from, the people that I know. It gave me a whole new appreciation for my life that I didn't have before I left for high school. I found out that it was something wonderful and that a lot of people would love to have the life I have.

JMJ: My grandfathers, on both sides of my family, were extremely hard workers, came from nothing and built their own companies They were very successful at the end of their lives and extremely well-respected in the community. I couldn't think of two greater people to look up to, or to have as role models. In my opinion, they couldn't be great men if they didn't have the great women. For example, my dad's father depended on my grandmother so much in their 63 years together — he depended on her like oxygen — he died last year of loneliness.

KJR: What do you see as the future of ranching?
JMJ: Keeping up with the times, keeping up with technology, keeping up with what the consumer wants. You have to market your beef to the little deli in Boston, and make sure that it is easy for the corporate housewife. She doesn't want all that preparation. A lot of people just don't have time anymore.

KJR: So how do you, as an individual rancher, produce a product to fit their needs?
JMJ: First of all we keep a lot of data. We record the details of our calves from the day they're born until the day they're slaughtered. We take everything from birth weights, to weaning weights, to yearling weights, all measurements, recording EDP's, expected progeny differences on all our cattle. We take carcass measurements on all our cattle. Yet, even with all this progressive technology we're still getting the same prices that we got back in 1978. How can you run a ranch in 1998 with prices that are 20 years old?

KJR: What goals do you have for the ranch?
JMJ: As far as our cattle operation is concerned, and especially our seed stock operation, our main goal is to provide a better quality animal for the consumer. That's the bottom line. Providing a better product, and we're going to all available technology, because technology can advance us faster and further than ever before. Technology is really coming into the mainstream of ranching today. We love it here and we want to stay here, so we're trying to do the right thing.

Moon Ranch

Interview with Jon and Jackie Means at the ranch headquarters at Van Horn, Texas on May 13, 1998. The Means family has ranched in the Davis Mountains since John Z. and Exa Gay Means, Jon's great-grandparents, moved there in 1884; his mother Barbara Means still lives on the ranch. Jon and Jackie have three children, Mary Elizabeth, Sarah Anne and Cole Cowden Means, II.

KJR: Is the Means family an old ranching family?

JOM: My great grandfather had four sons and three daughters. They had children and most of the descendants of those families are still ranching today. The home ranches are still together. Our family has been broad minded in terms of planning for the future and for the succession of these ranches. A great example is how they divided up my cousin's ranch north of Silver City, New Mexico. The map made for the ranch shows that they went to every quarter and separated it out where each one of them could get a watering. It illustrates a very amicable settlement. They went even right down through the middle of a tank, so both could have water. It is the same way here. We're ranch people. My grandmother was a ranch girl, who married my grandfather, M.O. 'Bug' Means. My mother is a ranch girl and is still a partner in this ranch. Jackie is the first girl in this family that wasn't raised on a ranch.

JAM: After 20 years, I guess I am now.

JOM: In 1980 we set up the Means Ranch Company as a partnership involving Jackie and me in partnership with my mother, Barbara Means and my sister Kay Harbison and brother-in-law Doug Harbison, who live in St. Louis. I have been through five ranch settlements. It's a pretty sobering experience.

KJR: How has this ranch grown over the generations?

JOM: In this area water is paramount. In the beginning when this ranch was put together there were only about four waterings. Today, on the same land we have about 150 waterings. The fact that this country is watered is what makes it what it is. My ancestors also started to control the brush and put up the fences. Early on they root-plowed a lot of this country and tried scraping the brush off with a maintainer, which didn't work too well. Root-plowing this country is challenging. If they root-plowed too deep and they lost their moisture. Everything had to be just right when you root-plowed. If it rained at the right time that seed would sprout and germinate, if it didn't the seed would dry up, die, and it's back to nothing.

JOM: They also drilled a lot of water wells with storage and troughs. Since then, we've done a lot of pipe lining and now fast line. Fast line was developed for the oil fields. You don't have to put it together by hand. It comes in a spool that you literally roll out. We put in four miles of fast line in one day. It's critical in this country. We order one-thousand foot rolls for how ever many miles we want. It will come on spools, we'll make connections and have it done in a matter of hours. On a leased ranch we lay this on top of the land. Usually we bury it with a ripper just like they put in cable for telephone. To me, it's been one of the biggest things that's happened to ranching in our generation.

JAM: Unique to this area is the size of the land out here. We run a cow per every sixty acres. So we think in terms of miles of pipeline, not feet.

JOM: We still use a plain old windmill, but with a submersible and a generator. You can pump water for a lot of cattle. And with the storage the strategic lines are connected to together by fast line. It is water that makes this country. Also if you can distribute water, then you don't have a big concentration of cattle in one area which protects the forage.

KJR: What cattle do best in this country?
JOM: This is the highland Hereford area of Texas. That's why this area is famous for Hereford cattle, but our family has raised Angus cattle for 60 years. We have used some Brahman bulls on these cattle to produce a black F-1 female, which is probably the best cow for this country that you can have. They hustle a little bit more and get around a little bit better. It's their hybrid vigor.

JAM: Black cattle are very popular right now. There is a big market for them.

JOM: We decided to keep our Angus cows for several reasons. One, we've worked extremely hard on their genetics for a long time. We sell all the heifers we can raise. On this ranch, our Angus cattle have performed better.

JAM: We have a niche market. We sell a load at a time. A few bulls here and few heifers there, and it makes a big difference in the overall profit picture. We don't sell all of our steers on video in one day. If we're going to sell on video, we do them in different lots to take advantage of market ups and downs.

KJR: Jackie, how did you come to this ranch?
JAM: He made me an offer I couldn't resist. I grew up in El Paso, went to college in the Northeast and received a degree in economics. I returned to El Paso and worked for IBM in sales for a few years. I met Jon through a family friend. When we finally decided to get married, I moved down here. I thought about it long and hard before I made that

decision — it was a big change. I was not a blushing bride of nineteen. Interestingly, I do think that that my business background has been helpful to us.

JOM: I think Jackie sees some things more real realistically than I do.

JAM: I don't get emotional.

JOM: I'm more spontaneous. Jackie can say, now let's think about this.

JAM: I have taken over the administration and book work.

JOM: We have an office in town.

JAM: I think I've become the sounding board. He and I arrive at our decisions together. Jon's mom has always been very supportive, very hands off. She doesn't want to be involved in the decisions. She prefers to enjoy the ranch.

JOM: My grandmother came here and she was a businesswoman. She was a ranch girl from Midland and came when she was 17 years old. I grew up, here, with my grandparents. They spoiled me. I lived right here and was very close to my grandmother. My grandfather died when I was nine, so she was widowed a long time. When I'd go out on the ranch she'd say: "Okay, I'm going to ask you questions, and you'd better be able to answer them. If you don't, I'm going to send you back." And she did. She was strong, too. That's one thing I learned from her, you make a decision.

JAM: What we have to do has changed so much in 20 years. When I first came here Jon did a lot more going out on the ranch. A lot more riding, more time in his pickup. As we get older our business gets more complicated, more sophisticated as it grows. He spends more time behind his desk and on the phone. I have too. When I was first here, I rode around the ranch, went every place he went. Today we have more business, and of course, we have a family. I don't really know how it's evolved that we're so overwhelmed

by our business. When I first came here it wasn't nearly this complex. It seems to me we were more cowboys and now we're managers.

JOM: When we first got married, we didn't have workers comp. We didn't have insurance for our employees and all the paperwork of today.

KJR: How many children do you have?
JAM: We have two daughters, Lizzie who's seventeen and Sarah who's eight, and a son Coley who's fifteen. We keep a house in town so the kids can go to school there. They're very active in sports and Student Council and all. They help with the branding and with shipping. On the weekends, when they are here, our son in particular really loves it. Anytime he can jump in the truck with dad he goes. We both feel that it's really important for all of the children to be involved. Even if the girls feel they don't want to pursue this way of life or this business, they need to know what goes into it to be good partners with our son if he decides to stay and ranch. They've been here and done the work. They know the struggles and the heartaches.

JOM: And the joys.

KJR: As the fifth generation, what do you see as the future for the next generation?
JAM: I have a different perspective on this than Jon since I'm not emotionally tied to the heritage. I have learned to love this life. I enjoy the serenity and the beauty and the freedom, the autonomy of our way of life. I see great virtues in it. On the other hand, there are real drawbacks to living out here. By drawbacks I mean it is difficult. It's hard to be 38 miles from a gallon of milk or 3 hours each way to a major city. Education is an issue. Socialization is difficult. I want my children to choose this life because they really want it, with their eyes wide open as to what they're facing. It's difficult to educate them without putting great stresses and strains on your family. If they want to ranch — great.

We want to help them do that, but we want them recognize the negatives, the down-sides.

JOM: Some of the most miserable people I know are ranching because they thought they had to and they hate every minute of it. Then, turn that coin around and some of the most fulfilled people I know are ranchers because they love it.

KJR: Do you have outside help?

JOM: We have been blessed with longtime, stable employees, who are like an extended family. Miguel Barraza began working for my great-grandfather at fourteen and remained until age eighty-two. He and his brother, Chuy Barraza, took pride in having worked for four generations of the Means family. My father hired Alejandro Hinojos who has been with us for forty-six years. Two of his boys are still with us. When we're gone we don't ever worry. We never worry about the children. And we all live right here together. It's a very good relationship. Everybody respects everybody else.

KJR: Does the ranch have outside income?

JAM: The ranch company has made it's own way. It pays it's own way.

JOM: The ranch company leases the land from the people, pays all the bills, pays the help, the insurance, owns the cattle, buys the pickups. It's the operating entity. I get a salary from the ranch company. Jackie gets a salary from the ranch company. Jackie and I don't own a cow. We own three geldings that were cutting horses. Everything we have is in a partnership with somebody else and it's fine. We get dividends from the ranch company. The ranch company has made some investments on its own, and they are the ranch company investments. It's all been generated from the hoof of a cow. In a humble way I'm proud of that.

KJR: What is unique about ranching in this country?

JOM: We can get no rain, or we can get thirty-two inches in a year. We have to ranch very conservatively. Ranching is an art, not a science. You have to ranch very conservatively in West Texas. This is a real strong country, but a very unpredictable country. We know when it's supposed to rain, but we don't know when it's going to rain. We could get all the rain in one month. The old timers say it's supposed to rain the fourth of July. Most of our rain comes in August, September and October. We don't have that much feed, but what we have is strong. Cattle do really well here. This country has a lot of variety. We've got grass. We can have a good weed crop. We've got a lot of different varieties of grass. All of those are very positive. The negative is the rainfall.

JAM: We are conservative in all aspects of our ranch. We know we're going to have hard years, and we've got to plan for them. We work at saving for the bad times.

JOM: An ideal situation for us is to have enough money in the bank to run the ranch the next year. Agriculture can support operating debt, but agriculture can't support a lot of long-term debt. When you look at the returns and you know what interest is you have to manage carefully. We gross a tremendous amount of money sometimes. But the net is not there.

JAM: I've always admired Jon's desire to improve and move forward. He's a confident risk taker. I'm much more conservative and think it's my job to ask the tough questions first.

KJR: What about innovations?

JOM: Besides fencing, water, pens and traps, I'd say that what has changed this ranch more than anything is the genetics of a cow. We use EPD's, the expected progeny differences, as a road map to where we want to go genetically.

JAM: The information that cattle producers have about the genetics and performance of their cattle from the time they're born until they're over the meat counter, has improved tremendously in 20 years. They have more genetic history on Angus cattle than they do any other breed. And since we have Angus cattle, we take advantage of this and it pays.

JOM: What we're selling is food for the consumer. We have to know what our product is. We have to know exactly how to produce the best product consistently — produce a predictable product. Also, how to most efficiently feed these cattle for the best results. Feeding is a 'dry matter conversion.' The smaller amount of feed and the more pounds they gain. We're working towards an animal that will convert to 5 x 5's; they're going to gain 5 lbs. a day and convert 1 to 5 on dry matter. If we can get to there, we are feeding them a lot less feed, it's taking a lot less time, and they'll still grade and yield. What they're trying to do, ultimately, is that a steer raised on Means Ranch Company is identified as Lot No. 739, Tag No. 8044. When that comes across the shelf at Safeway, they'll know exactly where that steer was raised, how he was handled, who killed him, who packaged the meat and where he is in the Safeway store in El Paso. This information will be on the box.

JAM: Jon has plans for selling every head at a premium.

JOM: One of my goals is that every female produced here as replacement sells for a premium. Then sell as many bull calves as possible for a premium, by the head. Make the steers have such a good genetic package they do well on anybody's grid and command a premium in the beef. We are looking to create a superior product—to raise the bar as high as we can.

KJR: How have your ranch improvements impacted your wildlife?
JOM: On this ranch, we have deer, antelope, quail, dove, javelina and some elk. We don't derive much income from our hunting. This is not a ranch that lends itself to large number of hunters.

JAM: The wildlife out here is under tremendous pressure from the drought. However, as far as the deer around the house, they thrive because they live on our yard.

KJR: What legacy would you like to leave for future generations?
JOM: Well, I'd just like people to think of us as real cow people, real ranch people. Beyond reproach, with integrity. I'd like our children, to have the work ethic. Whatever they're going to do, they have to work. They need to learn it here. Regardless of what our children do, I want them to know how to do a good job.

JAM: Something that I noticed about kids growing up in this environment is that they can inherit an asset that is worth a lot of money. Theoretically, if you put it on the market, you could get a lot of money for it. There's a tendency to think that they have a lot of money. I think it's really important for our children to have a real good understanding of the need to live within your means. It would be easy to spend out this ranch. Whatever asset they have, they need not to spend it up. That's just good business. That's just smart.

JOM: You could go to the bank and borrow as much money as you want to against this Ranch. They'll loan it to you. My granddad said, "You can carry it out of there a hell of a lot easier than you can carry it back."

JOM: A philosophy of ours is that this year's already done. You need to be ranching for next year and the next year after that. A ranch is so slow. It takes nine months to even conceive a calf. You put a bull on a cow and you've got nine months 'til the calf is born.

Then you've got another nine months before you do anything with him. If you choose to feed, we're talking about twenty-one months before you ever see a payday on an animal. I think that we need to be very good at long range planning and keep our goals way out in front of us. Also, we have to do the small things better than anybody else. Lots of people in ranching do the big things the same and probably do them right, but there are a lot of little things that we need to do better.

JOM: I'm real big on some of the old ways. Those old people knew what they were doing. They spent a lot of time on horseback. They knew what the cattle were eating. They knew if that cow was bred. They knew what kind of calves she had. Now it's to the point where everything is in a hurry. We still brand with the wagon here, sometimes. I feel there are a lot of things that we've lost, as far as being real cowmen, by not using the old traditions when they will work for us today.

JAM: I think that Jon does a good job of blending tradition with a modern ranch business. But at the same time, this ranch isn't just a business. This is different; this is a way of life, as well as a business. There's a balance there to be achieved. Yes, we want to be profitable. Yes we want to have a good sound business and be able to preserve it for the future. At the same time it is important that it be enjoyable. That it be a vehicle for preserving our family unity and rearing children who are responsible and who have basic values that will serve them well through life.

JOM: As long as God leaves me here it is my goal to be a good steward of these lands and to leave them in better shape for the next generation.

Moorhouse Ranch

Interview with John and Tom Moorhouse, at the home of their mother, Lucille Moorhouse in Benjamin, Texas, on May 24, 1998. Their grandfather ran cattle in the Indian Nations before moving to King County, Texas, about 1906. Their parents, Togo and Lucille Moorhouse, bought the headquarters ranch near Benjamin. Togo died in 1995 and Lucille still lives in Benjamin.

KJR: How is the Moorhouse Ranch managed today?

TM: All four of us, Ed, John, Bob and I are directors of the Moorhouse Ranch Company, although Bob is also the manager of the Pitchfork Ranch, and Ed handles real estate in Dallas. We have directors' meetings bimonthly where we make the major decisions. John and I co-manage and divide the daily responsibilities. John does the livestock buying and selling, handles the wheat-field cattle and the farming. I handle the leased ranches and cowboy crew of men that work for us.

KJR: How many lease ranches do you have now?

TM: We have about six leases.

JM: We've done quite a bit of expanding. We've bought several small places around this area in addition to the leased ranches. We've carried on what my dad started — we

worked with him for many years and have expanded what he started. We just have commercial cattle and try to raise good ones. We don't sell any replacement cattle. Tom is the bull buyer.

TM: We've gone mostly to black bulls — Angus bulls because today the packers like black cattle. They seem to marble better. John's always said that until now the only way you were paid for genetics was in the added production that they do while you own them and not particularly when you sell them. That's changing, so we're going to watch our genetics closer.

JM: We've been feeding our cattle quite a bit. We raise good cattle, but it's a game of economics. We do what pays. Essentially, our operation is three segments: the cow/calf business, the yearling business, and farming business. Tom looks after the cow/calf operation. All these leased ranches are cow/calf operations. On our home ranch we have about 13,000 acres of wheat that is for feeding yearlings. We wean calves and buy calves to bring home on the wheat. We're farming for the cattle. We plant wheat to graze, but when it starts growing in the spring we can get off a part of it for harvest and double up grazing on the rest of it. Oat fields provide hay for the company horses. Whether we cut more wheat or less depends on markets. If the wheat is high we try to cut more. If we can buy yearlings reasonably in late winter and put weight on them—sometime we graze out more. The markets determine the course we take.

TM: Markets and weather. Some years, if it's a good year, you have more wheat than you can graze. Some years are dry. The beauty of wheat is the flexibility. We can graze it out, harvest it or bail it. Wheat makes very good hay if you cut it down right.

KJR: What's your biggest obstacle in this country?
JM: The biggest obstacle here is the same as everywhere: getting enough rain. The second obstacle is brush. We're blessed with surface water right here at home. We have

good tanks and we keep our old tanks cleaned out. However, the other leased ranches are for the most part windmill water, well water, and that's a problem. Tom says the only thing cheap about a windmill is the wind. All the rest of it's high priced. The second obstacle in this country is brush and brush control. If you take markets and weather out, then brush is the biggest obstacle in this country.

KJR: Do you use outside help in the daily operation?

TM: We have two crews: the cowboy crew and the farm crew. We have foremen on the leased ranches. So we have about 10 or 12 guys that work as cowboys and about four that work on the farm.

KJR: How do you decide if a leased ranch is going to work for you?

JM: Every deal is different. We recently leased the Shannon Ranch down at Big Lake, and that's a long way from home. We are putting a lot of confidence in the man managing it, because he's been there 12 years and he's a good, capable man. At the rest of these ranches, Tom calls the shots. The decision is based on the numbers. All the numbers have to stack up, the cost of production for that ranch. The Shannon is a cow/calf deal so we had our yellow pad out and went to figuring and it just seemed like a workable venture. Those cows stay there and we'll wean their calves and bring them up here to winter them on wheat and sell them in the spring.

KJR: What innovations do you think you've brought to ranching?

JM: We're not really innovators but we are progressive. We're low-overhead operators. We have no outside income, no oil. We don't have an airplane or a helicopter. Tom takes that wagon out in the spring and the fall and sleeps on the ground in the old traditional ranching way.

TM: We change as we think we need to, but we're not the kind that's running around trying to find some newfangled way. Everything we do has been tested and works pretty well. Our dad was progressive. He stayed in tune with the markets and what was going on, but he was also a traditionalist. We're doing like he did except that we're a little bigger.

KJR: What do you think you're going to need to do differently in the next 20 years?
JM: I've got some question about the beef business. The way it is right at the moment, it doesn't look very good to me. We're losing our market share and it's reflecting on our livelihood. Competitive meats are one of the major problems with our market today. I think our old business will be here forever, but it may take some innovative moves, in the future. We have joined a beef alliance with other ranchers to merchandise our cattle together — it's basically a cooperative.

TM: I have some concern that the market doesn't seem to stay where it needs to be and the overhead keeps going up which puts a little bind on us. But I think that things will eventually work out, because I do think beef is here to stay. The last two or three years have been a bad disappointment. We've been through a down cattle cycle and we thought this was a comeback year and it's not.

JM: Our plans are to continue raising beef. We'll adjust, or do what we need to do to stay in the business. To me, we live in three Americas — the East Coast and the West Coast and then the breadbasket of America. What you hear on CNN has nothing to do with the way we live out here. Most of America is not even aware of what our lives are like. Today our economy is technology driven, not production driven. I think this old country is going to have to get good and hungry before we get back to agriculture again.

KJR: Do you have hunting on your ranches?
JM: Yes, but we don't capitalize on hunting. We do lease it out by the acre, but we don't personally take in hunters. We are going to change that, however, because of the economy.

TM: Nowadays, the hunting has to be considered on all ranches whether you're buying, selling or leasing.

JM: We'd rather have a little less money and put our efforts into the ranching business and not the hunting business.

KJR: What improvements have you made environmentally?
TM: If you're a rancher, you're an environmentalist. You want your cattle to be fat and your water to be clean and the country to be good. I like the natural habitat and don't want anything to happen to it. Today I wouldn't shoot anything if I wasn't going to eat it, and I don't shoot much of that because I'd rather eat beef anyway.

KJR: Have you seen much change in the wildlife?
TM: Yes, for sure. We used to have very few deer and now we have lots of deer, whitetail. I remember the first turkey I ever saw out there, and now we have flocks of turkey pass through although they don't stay because we don't have any big trees.

JM: We have quail and geese. Wild hogs have moved in here in recent years, and we have an abundance of them. I really think the wild hogs have hurt the quail population. Hogs have a powerful sense of smell and they can smell those quail eggs. They nearly did away with blue quail, in our country.

KJR: What do you see for the future of ranching?
JM: Our plans are to continue raising beef. Instead of just plopping beef out on the counter, we're going to have to find out exactly what the consumer wants and sell it to her. People have changed, diets have changed and we'll do whatever it takes to stay in the cattle business.

KJR: How do you address the public's perception of ranchers?

TM: You have the East Coast and the West Coast and they don't have a clue what the ranching business is like. They view ranching as a pleasure lifestyle. To us it's a serious business, just as serious as any other business in the world. It's the bottom line that we're interested in. Some people say, we have a good way of life and we do if everything is working. But when the cycle is down you are in a survival period, which is very stressful, because you're trying to survive. It's not a matter of how much money you're going to make, it's a matter of are you going to survive. You may get a break of a year or two, then you can spend a little money on improvements — brush control, or buildings or whatever. But when the down cycle returns, it's back to survival — hanging in there until it gets a little better. I don't think the general public understands that ranching, at its best, is a poor return on the investment.

JM: It's just not a lucrative business.

KJR: So what keeps you in it?

TM: We like it. I'm hooked. I'm fifty-two years old and don't know anything else.

JM: It gets in your blood. I understand the farming and ranching, and I don't think I'd like a lot of other things. I think the good Lord put me here to do what I'm doing.

TM: That's how I feel — I do think that some of my genetics is the cattle business. I think I'm turned that way.

KJR: How would you like your ranching operation to be perceived?

TM: Well, we'd like to be recognized just the way it is. It's a business with a lot of risk to it and a lot of hard work without much return on the investment. And, we would like to be known as the environmentalists that we are.

KJR: If money or labor were not a problem, would you ranch any differently?
TM: If we had plenty of money, we would make more improvements, and we would pay our workers more because they're like us. They could make more money elsewhere, but they're in it because they like it. Those would be the two things we would do — ranch improvements and pay better wages.

JM: I wish our business was a little more lucrative, but honestly, I don't know if it would change anything. We'd have a little better return and we'd be building faster than what we are. But I don't think we'd change anything other than to operate better.

TM: I can tell you a story: My dad at one time worked for a dollar a day and he always kept one pair of boots for work and one pair of boots for dress. He always kept a little bit of whiskey, and that was just about the extent of his luxuries. That was in the '20's and the '30's. He died when he was 90, and he had a pair of boots that he worked in; a new pair of boots that he went to church in, and he had a little whiskey, and that was just the extent of his luxuries — and he was worth considerably more then, than he was in the '20's and '30's. So his outlook on spending was putting it back into the ranch. John and I are probably a good bit like that — it doesn't take a whole lot to keep us happy, as long as the market and the weather are good.

Powell Ranches

Interview with Jimmie and Nancy Powell at their office in San Angelo, Texas, on May 11, 1998. Powell family ranching history dates back to 1885 as a homesteading operation. The Powells have two daughters, Lorrie Uhl and Victoria Jackson and their families.

KJR: When did you return to the family ranching operation?

JP: In 1954, I came from the service and went into the ranching business with my twin sisters. We operated as a partnership through college and the early years. After I came back from the service we divided the properties. Nancy also came from a ranch family. The operation has grown about ten fold since we started, when we married in 1960.

KJR: What have you done to make ranching work for you?

JP: What we have done to make the ranching business profitable goes back to our earlier education, in business school. You learn that if you invest, you want to diversify. If you want to be successful you want to maintain a core investment without it deteriorating. So we have diversified. Besides lands, we have invested in energy operations as well as banking and other high-tech operations that were minuscule in the beginning and had opportunity to grow. The operation has become successful as a result of segmented management practices. These involve range management, which is control of noxious plants and non-beneficial trees and bushes; management of livestock through genetic selection and production records; management of the range with a high-intensity, low-frequency grazing system, patterned after one I saw in South Africa in the 1960s; and management of nutrition, a very important factor. We have analyzed the grasses on the properties that we operate over a period of about 12 to 15 years. From that, we have formulated minerals that will supplement these forages that the livestock graze. There-fore, this allows the livestock to exist at a peak performance level, so that they maximize their calf crops, lamb crops and produce the heaviest offspring that they can.

JP: The grazing practices were adopted as a result of my visit to South Africa where I saw a high-intensity, low-frequency system operate on the deserts of South Africa. A very fascinating program that Dr. Howell had established 30 years prior. He had a going enterprise with stocking rates far beyond any of the neighboring properties. I found this to be the case when we made the investment to cut our pastures into smaller ones and put more watering on the property. We were able to approximately double the live stock production on the ranch. This has been, coupled with these other management prac-tices, one of the reasons that our operation has been profitable. This system we use is a rectangular system, basically, with watering on every quarter section. The livestock do not have to walk to find water, nor do they have to walk to find food. When they finish grazing and watering, they lay down and as a result retain the weight that they gain. Rather, than using the energy to walk for water. That's the reason that we have heavier calves when we wean them than a system that requires less water and constant grazing. Philosophically, it's much better, but it is more costly to initiate. Although it repays itself in a very rapid way.

JP: Brush control is necessary. In our country, mesquite utilizes 2,800 lbs. of water to produce one pound of forage, and it is non-beneficial. If you eliminate mesquite, you triple the amount of grass, because grass only requires about 750 lbs. of water to grow

one pound of grass. Those are the mid to the tall grasses. The shorter grasses don't require that much. You create a greater inventory of grasses with which to graze your livestock, and as a result, you can put more livestock on the property, still improve the grasses and multiply your species. We've demonstrated that that can be done. You can also go through drought periods like we're in now much easier. Because we have old grasses with a large root system, a little rain will green them up. They will become strong and provide forage that otherwise wouldn't be provided with a plant that has a smaller root system.

KJR: What are the factors that make a ranch successful today?
JP: A factor that makes a ranch successful is in treating it as a business operation, not as a strict agricultural operation where you only produce and pay no attention to the markets. You have to take into consideration all aspects of the livestock operation, beginning with genetics and going all the way through to the study of the markets and trends that develop. Then you know the best time to sell, you know what genetics produce better in your area, you know what production practices will develop heavier weights and the better livestock.

KJR: What breeds of cattle are you using to do that?
JP: We're using the Angus breeds that were originally raised for human consumption. Angus cows with a Hereford bull. Utilizing our registered herd of Herefords we raise Hereford bulls and put them on the Angus cows. The consumer is becoming a more selective buyer of beef, and that's one of the reasons that branded beef is succeeding today. I think that trend is going to increase. We are interested in investing in a certified Hereford beef program, which is just an extension of what we're doing. We're raising beef. Now we want to go directly to the consumer, if we can. This is another aspect of diversifying in the investment field. The consumer is going to make the market much

more lucrative if she can consistently buy what she likes. We want to be on the upper end of the scale so that we can insure the success of our operation in the future.

KJR: What obstacles have been overcome to get to this point?
JP: The history of the livestock business has been that of overcoming obstacles. The generations before us had problems that they solved for us. Such as, discovering underground water, controlling predators both animal and human so we don't have those problems today. The problems we do have, today, are not so much environmental as they are governmental, the resistance of a government to a way of life that is harmful to that way of life. Our way of life is not going to make you immensely wealthy like a high-tech business, but it can provide a fine living and a way of life your children can come home to if they choose. Our obstacles are how do you get government to allow an environment that enhances agriculture and encourages young people to stay in agriculture. Government regulation, taxes and wasteful practices do not encourage young people to stay in agriculture. That's the reason we have less than two percent of our population in agriculture today, and we're going to have fewer in the future unless government changes.

JP: Another problem is financing agricultural operations. Today, banks are consolidating, merging. They're looking at the bottom line. They think that agriculture is more risky to lend to than other operations like a corporation that sells Coca-Cola and has a large cash flow, and innovative marketing. They can increase their cash flow immensely. Agriculture does not have that ability. It also does not have ability to repay its debts as timely as corporate structures do. Today lending corporations, or lending entities, that historically have been agricultural lenders, are changing to more of a corporate lender in order to reduce the risks that they perceive. Therefore, requiring a more precise operation. Agriculture is not a precise operation simply because of the nature of weather and the lack of consistency in production and markets. You have more risk. Lending is a big factor. You're not seeing many young people coming into agriculture simply because lenders don't lend to them. They don't have the ability to borrow that which is required. Young people just don't have that at this point. The banking industry is not interested in it. So agriculture is lacking available financing.

KJR: Do you two share in the management of your businesses?
NP: We've always worked together and lived right there and tried to do what we thought was best on a daily basis. Jimmy, of course, is the prime manager and mover and shaker, and I'm the light heart. Early on, I handled the bills, the check writing and the books. Now we've moved into the computer age and I'm not quite as involved in that.

JP: The operation has grown to the extent that it takes a couple of secretaries to keep all the paperwork flowing.

KJR: Do you have extra outside help?
JP: We have several families that work in various places.

KJR: What is their level of responsibility?
JP: Well, we have a management plan as you know. Their responsibility encompasses as much of that management plan as they will embrace. Now, we have a manager that supervises the foremen on the various properties and that manager sees that management plan is carried out and any modification to it is in consultation with Nancy and me. We also, of course, are looking at that management plan to see that it's carried out on a daily basis, weekly basis and so forth. A plan will work only so well as the personnel who are operating it. We have good people working for us.

KJR: Do you have outside income?
JP: Well, as I stated before, diversification has been one of the tenets of our business philosophy, so that today, outside income will equal approximately 50% of our total. But

the ranches are still self-sustaining. With ranch income we invested in other areas and developed those areas as well as the ranching. Investments have been made specifically for the purpose of maximizing returns, not necessarily from agriculture, but from other areas. Owning land has been the basic asset for this enterprise, and you own land because it will return income, not only from livestock, but also from energy as well as recreation. We utilize all of those areas.

KJR: What innovations have you introduced?

JP: I suppose, to some extent, we've set an example for those who would like to increase their productivity. We've written plans and developed this process for the extension service to demonstrate to others that you can increase production by a high-intensity, low-frequency system. You have to invest in fencing to create more pastures, and invest in waterings for more abundant water. We've also, through our experimentation and data process, accumulated an immense amount of information concerning the food value of the plants that grow in this area through different periods. Drought periods, wet periods, winter, summer, spring and fall. As a result we've formulated minerals that supplement the grasses for their deficiencies and allow the livestock to produce to the peak of performance. Those minerals are being supplied by one or two mineral manufacturers formulated from the information that they gain from us.

JP: We've been perfectly open for any who desired information. Annually, we host the Texas Christian University Range Program. It is a two-year ranch course for youngsters who want to go into the ranching business. We have a written agenda that describes our operation and they can take it and use it if they want to, or learn from it what they'd like. If we find something that someone else is doing that is beneficial, we sure adopt that, or try to.

KJR: How are you preparing to move into the new millennium?

NP: The new century will require, as the last has, that the operation make a profit and utilize all potential to its fullest, which may require changing the livestock management program to adjust to the demand. Adjusting genetics. It will probably lead to greater recreational needs for the general public. It may require the rancher to maintain ownership of their product from production all the way to the final marketing to the consumer. In order to be more profitable, because there's so much middle ground. It will also give you better control of what you're producing. We've always attempted to improve the property so that it's more productive and attractive each year than it was the year before. That is a constant conservation effort. We need to preserve it for the future generations, so we can continue to feed and clothe the world. We have to be stewards of the bounty the Lord has given us. We need to be aware of the developing changes in business and the political environment so that we can favorably influence them.

JP: Earlier we discussed the influence that government has had on our business. As a result of that, Nancy and I, both, have been quite active in industry organizations in an attempt to influence legislation, as well as the business environment. Not every cowman or sheepman is of a nature to organize. He's always been independent and wants to take care of his own in the way he sees fit. But there's always going to be somebody slipping up on the other side. We need organizations to do what needs to be done that the individual can't do alone.

KJR: What do you see in the future of your ranching operation?

JP: For thousands of years the individual has had, basically, three needs. They've had a need for food, for clothing and for shelter. We're producing one of those needs and we'll always have that need. There'll never be an end to it. The question will be whether or not the rancher will be remunerated for the production he sells to those individuals that have that need.

KJR: What legacy would you like to leave for your future generations?

JP: Well, if someone were to look back on our operation, I'd hope that they could say that the operation was structured and managed so that our children are able to operating at the peak of efficiency and make the most of that agricultural operation.

NP: We've been stewards of what we have and improved it to the best of our ability, knowing that it was a gift from God. We had that opportunity to use what He created and hope that we can enhance it to the fullest and pass it on so that it will be useful to the next generation.

JP: The people who are genuinely interested in agriculture will become better educated about how to produce in agriculture. A free enterprise system operates where other people learn from those who are successful. Those who are successful are very grateful to have the opportunity to teach those who want to be more successful, want to create markets and a greater income.

Ryan Ranches

Interview with Nolan and Ruth Ryan at their office in Alvin, Texas, on July 14, 1998. In addition to his brilliant baseball career, Nolan has been involved with cattle since he was a boy. Nolan and Ruth bought their first ranch in 1972, and now run cattle on three ranches in South Texas.

KJR: When did you start raising cattle?

NR: As a youngster I would buy the bull calves from the local dairies and bottle feed them. I would raise them to weaning age and sell them as feeders. When I would accumulate enough money I started buying heifers. I finally had to sell them because of my sports interests in high school. That's where the seed was planted and I always wanted to get back into it, and baseball gave me that ability.

KJR: When were you able to return to the cattle business?

NR: In 1972 I bought a set of thirty-two heifers and then I went back the following year and bought another twenty-four heifers. So really in a two-year period that was the start of my herd. The nucleus of those cattle produced until they were 18 years old.

KJR: Ruth, were you raised in the city or the country?

RR: I was raised right here in Alvin, so I can't call myself a city girl, but I'm not a country girl either.

NR: She's got a lot more country in her than she takes credit for.

RR: I love to help them at the ranch.

NR: Our life together has been a partnership, whether in the cattle operation or in baseball. She's done a lot of things in ranching that she never thought she would. She has pulled calves and hauled hay. But it needed to be done. It's all part of our life experience and we enjoy it.

RR: We have been married 31 years. I've always appreciated our time together, maybe because of baseball we were separated half the time. I felt that in the winter, when we were together, it didn't matter where we were or what we were doing. The fact that he was happy on the ranch, that made me happy.

NR: I think if you asked our kids about our ranching operation, they'd all tell you it's a family operation and they're thrilled about being in a position that they can share that. They enjoy it and look forward to it and they help us a lot. When we work cows or haul hay, when we need the help from everybody, they're always there and often their friends come too. We have Reid who is 26, Reese is 22 and Wendy is 21. Wendy and Reese are still in college. Reid has his degree in radio, TV, and film and hosts a show called, "Fishing Texas," that airs on Fox Sports Southwest. He is also the president of a minor league baseball operation in Round Rock, Texas.

KJR: Is ranching what you always wanted to do?

NR: Yes, I always wanted to raise cattle and ranch. If I had my choice I'd live on the ranch on a day-to-day basis. Because of other things that require my time, and opportunities I have, I can not justify doing that just yet.

KJR: Ruth, how does ranch life fit for you?

RR: I love it probably because when he's there, he seems very at peace with himself and enjoys just being there. I love that for him because of all the years he spent playing baseball and the travel. I remember the first time in 1972 we went to look at this man's cattle. When we drove down there, I said, "Is this what you've been talking about. This is it? You think this is pretty?" I was very surprised because it was just so brushy, so wild. Over the years I've learned to love it. I love our ranch down there.

NR: That's the Ray Ranch in McMullen County, which is on the Nueces River. We're at the end of the road, and it's really wild down there. We run cows and heifers, and at times we run steers, depending on how much grass we have left.

RR: We built a beautiful ranch house and I love going there, and I know that he would probably retire and live there full time. I don't know whether I could live there, full time, although I love to be there. There is a little bit of difference there between us.

KJR: Where are your other two ranches?

NR: The China Grove Ranch here in Brazoria County is leased from an estate out of Houston. Gonzales County is where we started our first ranching operation and was the basis of our purebred operation for about ten years. Now that ranch is the nucleus of our cow-calf operation.

NR: I'm a believer in knowing what you have and following the cattle all the way through. A percentage of my heifers go back into the herd so I know how they perform. When I sell replacements I can honestly tell the buyer how they will perform because they perform for me. We take steers all the way through and we get the data back to analyze their performance. We want to know what we're doing and what we need to change. One of the problems we have in our business is of the fluctuation and quality of our product.

As producers we need to know what kind of product we are producing and what changes we need to make to fit the market.

KJR: What do you mean by the performance of cattle?
NR: The performance of the cattle is how they grow, develop, convert and grade. You have to be a good manager to maximize that. When you start doing things genetically, it's a slow process. It's a learning process.

NR: I think, one of the changes I have made in my cattle is fertility. I've paid a lot of attention to fertility and milking ability. Those two things keep you in the cow-calf business. You have to have fertile cattle, and they have to milk. The milking ability shows in the weaning weight of those calves, how fast and how big they grow. The fertility shows in the conception rate of the cows. Each year you look at the calf crop and see if you're making headway. I have always kept commercial cattle, but for about a ten year period my interest was in the purebred Beefmaster cattle. Finally I decided between the politics and money and time it takes to travel for a seed stock business that wasn't what I wanted to do.

KJR: What did you want to do?
NR: I'm a breeder of cattle. I wanted to raise cattle. I produce the same kind of cattle, but I'm not in it from a seed stock standpoint. I still like the Beefmaster breed and have probably 300 purebred cattle. That's where I produce a lot of my bulls and when I go out and buy a good bull to put on those cows I try and produce even better bulls. My interest has gone back to my commercial operation.

KJR: How do cattle adapt to this humid, hot country?
NR: It has to do with the humidity, heat and rainfall. What we have here is very fast-growing tall grass that does not have the nutritional value that short grass has, it's not very strong. Our cattle adapt really well. The rule of thumb is that you can take cattle

from east to west, but when you bring them from west to east, there has to be an adaptation period. They have to adapt to the climate. It's much harder on cattle to bring them to the Texas gulf coast. They don't perform as well going from west to east as they do from east to west.

KJR: How are you preparing for the new century?
NR: I think that there's going to be continued demands on us to produce a product that the consumer will accept, and we're going to have to become more cost efficient. We're going to have to produce a cheaper product. Our product is losing market share because of price. Chicken keeps making inroads. The pork people are doing better, and we've got to get better. As a consumer, when you go to a restaurant and spend money to buy a steak, it had better be what you want. I think we have the best product. We need to get the message out there and advertise our product. I'm a believer in being proactive, all the way, not being a defensive person. We need to go out there and tell it like it is.

KJR: Where did beef fit in your diet as a professional athlete?
NR: The one food I felt that was most important in my diet during my career as an athlete was red meat. I felt that beef offered more nutrition to me than anything else I ate. Now I'm certainly a believer in a balanced meal, and I believe in eating fruits and vegetables and nuts. That's all part of my diet routine. But I have always believed in eating beef.

KJR: Why doesn't the public recognize the importance of beef in their diet?
NR: I just don't believe that we're proactive enough. I think at times we do a little bit, but we need a solid advertising campaign and keep it up. We are always taking shots from people. People don't even know and they make comments with no information to back up what they're saying. As beef producers we need to tell it like it is.

KJR: What legacy would you like to leave for future generations?

NR: I'd like to see beef become more accepted and on a higher level so that we regain some of our market share. I'd like to pass my herd of cattle on to my children. I would like to know my kids appreciate the work I've done throughout my life to produce a genetically superior herd of cattle. A harrowing example of these efforts was during the drought of 1996. I agonized and anguished over those cattle. Financially I could not justify putting any more money into them; I was past the point of return. But I kept those cattle because of the genetics. I told Ruth, I had given 25 years to my breeding program. Those cattle are a reflection on my breeding program, and that's me. I had already paired them down to a nucleus. Everybody was in the same boat. It made economic sense just to load them up and sell them, but a part of me would have been gone. It had been my life work as an adult, and I wasn't prepared to give that up. Thank God it rained. Ruth will tell you, it changed my personality. It changed me.

RR: Severe depression.

NR: I dealt with it every waking minute. I tried everything I could think of — I moved cattle around and I bought hay from everywhere I could. I tried every thing. It was the biggest challenge I'd ever faced in the cattle business.

RR: It's not a business, it's a passion.

NR: We don't treat our cattle as you do your pets, because of the sheer numbers. But, I look at them every day that I'm on the ranch to see where we are with them, how they're progressing, their condition. It's an emotional attachment you have when you're a cow-calf operator. Those cows, they live with you day in and day out, and you have raised them from the first day they hit the ground to the day they become a producing cow in your herd. It is a passion. Every year I truly enjoy watching the calf crop develop. I get excited to watch them be born, to see what we have, then to grow them out and see how they perform, how they are improving. Each year I find that kind of excitement in every calf crop. Those cattle are part of our lives and we take care of them. And it's hard the day when they quit producing and you load them on the trailer and know what they're headed for. That aspect I don't like but it is necessary for the business.

KJR: Doesn't that passion for the cattle extend to the ranch environment?
NR: Absolutely. Ranching is a balancing act of taking care of your cattle, land and wildlife — being a good steward. As a rancher you don't want to do anything to your ranch to upset that balance — it is as important as how many dollars you can generate off your ranching operation.

RR: We could live anywhere in the world that we want. One day he was standing out at the ranch and he was just looking around and said, "Isn't this great?" I said, "What?" He says, "I can look in every direction on this horizon and not see one person." It's neat the way he can say, "Come on, let's go look at the cows." He'll drive around for hours and hours and just look and study. There's no telling what goes through his brain out there. He has a deep-rooted love for his cattle and ranch life.

NR; I have a passion for the cattle business. I will get up and speak to people about it because I'm committed to it. As a spokesperson, I am willing to do more, because it's my life.

Spade Ranches, Ltd.

Interview with Dub Waldrip, president and CEO, Spade Ranches, LTD., at the ranch office in Lubbock, Texas, on June 4, 1998. Isaac Ellwood, who pioneered the manufacture of barbed wire, bought the Renderbrook Spade Ranch in 1889. Today Jim McAdams is co-manger and the ranching operation includes the Chappell Spade in Tucumcari, New Mexico, and four leased ranches.

KJR: How long have you been with the Spade Ranches?

DW: Well, this month is 31 years with the Spade. Before that I was on the staff of Texas A&M. I was asked to come from College Station to Throckmorton County to organize and originate the first experimental ranch that we had in Texas in 1958. It was quite an endeavor. The Swenson Land & Cattle Company furnished the land and the cattle. A group of interested West Texas ranchers contributed enough money to provide the improvements that we needed to fence it, water it and get it started. Texas A&M furnished the research. It was a grazing nutrition study — an early ecological study in West Texas. After I'd been there about ten years, one of the contributors asked me to come and run the Spade. I've been here ever since.

KJR: What were you doing at Texas A&M?

DW: I was a professor in teaching and research. I had a Ph.D. in Range Ecology. My Bachelor degree was in Range Management and Forestry and my Master's degree was in Range Science.

KJR: Do you mean to tell me that you're one of the first environmentalists that is officially credentialed out here in the West?

DW: That's what's irritating. Nobody will pay any attention to me, especially the so-called environmentalists, because they think I'm biased. What really has bothered me through the years is that our ranch country is so much better than it was 50 to 60 years ago. It's unbelievable, the difference. You can't maintain range land without grazing. It can't be done, but nobody believes it.

KJR: What goals did you set up for the Spade that 31 years later, you're still doing?

DW: It took more people skills than it did ecological skills. We were the first among the first big ranches, to develop a pasture rotation, pasture rest grazing system on all the country and to set about cross breeding. We had what I call a four pasture, deferred rotation system. I had a series of systems on the ranch where we'd rest one while grazing three. Every four months or 120 days, you'd move out of one of those that you're grazing into the one you're resting. Over a 16-month period you've rested all of them at least four months, and over a three-year period you've rested all of them a full 12 months in sequential order. It's a lot easier to do than it is to explain. My cowboys thought I was crazy when we first started, and I probably was. But they really liked it because they didn't have to check water or salt or anything in the pasture that was being rested each time. That point I sold pretty well. They'd been grazing Hereford cattle since 1919 on the ranch and when we started adding new breeds, it took the year until we weighed the calves and saw the results. About that time, the feed lot industry was just coming into its own. To

engineer a better product, the only way to be paid for it was to finish them out and you could not do that with straight Herefords that we were raising.

KJR: Was the Spade one ranch at that time?

DW: No, there were two with different ownerships. The old original ranch, the Renderbrook Spade was organized in 1889, south of Colorado City. Then we had about 70 sections near Tucumcari, New Mexico, that belonged to Mr. Chappell, who was one of the owners of Renderbrook. After a while, we started expanding and when we'd get an opportunity, and it made more sense to lease than it did to buy. So we expanded up, at one time, to a little over 350,000 acres, and we're back down now to 325,000 acres.

KJR: Do you still lease ranches?

DW: We've still got the original two, plus four more. We run the two New Mexico ranches as one outfit and the Texas ranches as Spade Ranches, Ltd. They are run as one organization with one manager on each ranch.

KJR: When did Jim McAdams join the management team?

DW: I could tell that age was catching up with me and I've known Jim for 20 years. I watched him and liked what I saw in Jim. In 1991 I asked him if he'd come and help me run this outfit. We co-manage — I told him he could have all the responsibility and I'd take sole authority, and any credit.

KJR: What are the factors that make this ranch successful today?

DW: One thing is the people. We just never have any turnover to speak of. From a business standpoint, we probably would be better off if we did, but we have a lot of loyalty to the brand on our outfit. Another is the resource. I think the Rolling Plains of Texas is the best place in the United States to ranch — that's everything off the cap rock almost to I-35, say over to about Breckenridge. I think it is because your production costs are normally cheaper. Your wintering costs can be practically nil. We don't feed our cattle to speak of on any of the Texas ranches. If they can't get it from the grass, they just don't get it, by golly. Except, we supplement our bulls and replacement heifers to get them going. You don't feed them to fatten them. You just feed them to supplement what they're already getting.

KJR: Does outside income figure in to the Spade Ranch operation?
DW: No, only as recreation and hunting income.

KJR: What cattle do you raise, is it all commercial cattle?
DW: We've got four purebred herds, but we just raise bulls for our crossbred cows, We have a four breed, rotational crossbreeding program. We started with the original Herefords and I added Brown Swiss, now called Braunvieh, Angus, Simmental. I've tried almost everything but those are the four we've settled on. Everything that's sired with Hereford, spends their life with the Braunvieh. Everything sired by the Braunvieh spends their life with the Angus. Everything sired by the Angus is always bred to Simmental, and those offspring are crossed back to the Hereford. So we just go around in a circle. We get the full shot of hybrid vigor with each cross. If you have three crosses, you can't do it. Four you can and our calves weigh quite a bit.

KJR: What challenges do you have with your ranch country?
DW: Rainfall. Drought is a big issue. We've had some predator problems. I'd say production costs — labor, vehicles, housing and utilities — all of that goes into production costs are our biggest hurdle. Theoretically, you'd like to have one man look after a thousand cows, but if it takes 50,000 acres for those cows and calves, one man can't look after that.

KJR: Are you still using your rotational grazing today?
DW: Yes, it works for us. It doesn't matter what size your pastures are as long as they're four that are similar in carrying capacity. Because when you move the herd, you want it to

be in a pasture that it fits. When we turn these cows out, it takes them a while to be acclimated and find the water and make a home. We don't even like to call them up to feed them, because I feel like if I'm out honking the horn, then I'm calling cattle from other pastures too and disturbing them. I've found that they'll make a home for themselves if you'll just leave them alone and not disturb their daily activities by pulling cake out of the back of a pickup. You cannot overuse your country. You have to be sure there's plenty of grass there. It's been interesting, 25 years ago, when we'd have a bad drought, even though we reduced our numbers as the forage disappeared, it might take two to three years for it to come back. Now, we have enough strength, and vigor and health in our range that one or two good rains will bring it right back to where it was before. That comes from not asking it to do too much, when it is healing. Give the roots a chance to get stronger. Of course, the animals are going to eat the most desirable, the most palatable. Normally, they are the ones that are the highest on the succession scale, if you remove them the lower quality plants take their place. With this rotation system, you get a rest period every 12 months for four months. It gives those better plants a chance to recover, because under normal conditions they compete better than the lower quality plants anyway. If they didn't, they wouldn't be there. By getting out for four months, you've destroyed any spot grazing tendencies. We've spent a lot of time developing water so that we can more uniformly graze our pastures. If we can have water holes not more than a mile apart, we're in pretty good shape.

KJR: What has your rotational grazing done to improve the ranch for wildlife?
DW: Well, except for the bison, we've got more deer, turkey, quail and antelope than the Native Americans had.

KJR: What do you see as the challenges as we enter new millennium?
DW: I think our biggest problem is going to be keeping these large ranches in large units, as the heirs become more numerous. I think the general public — and this is just

being optimistic maybe — is becoming more interested in keeping these wild areas and not seeing them developed as the populations move in. The pendulum may be swinging as people get better informed, they may possibly become more sympathetic, and friendlier to our problems, than they have been the last 30 years. From the '60's on, we've seen a lot of folks, who are sincere, but not really informed. We may be overcoming part of that, but I'm not sure that we are. Maybe these folks are going to finally turn around and say: "Look, we've got to have those folks or we're not going to have any wild land." If they don't, you can imagine what will happen to the rural little towns and the tax base. Every ranch in the West has a private land unit to go with the public land allotment that feeds the wildlife, pays the taxes. It has the water and it supports the schools and the local utilities.

KJR: What about the future of the cattle industry?
DW: Well, they're either going to get better or they're going to get gone. I really wish that we didn't have so many misconceptions about human nutrition, balanced diets and red meat. It's like being in ecology. Nobody believes me. They don't want to, for some reason — it's not the "in" thing. There are only about nine poultry outfits in the United States and how many cattle ranches are there. Seventy-five to eighty percent have fewer than 50 calves. Now, how are you going to have a uniform product with that? Thank goodness it tastes as good as it does, and is as good for you. Basically all cattle people are more or less optimistic, but it bothers me that there's so much criticism of the folks that are trying to do something beneficial.

KJR: What kind of a legacy would you like to leave?
DW: I would like for folks to think that I left it in better shape than I found it. You have an innate interest or love in the land and you'd like to preserve it, take care of it. Not just for the sake of taking care of it, you'd like for it to be productive too. That's what I'd like people to say: "Well, old Dub, he did a good job taking care of his country." And, it is a

lot better than it was 98 years ago, in 1900. It's a whole lot better: the wildlife is better; the water's better; the livestock's better, the forage is a lot better, by golly. I told Jim that the main thing is to be sure that he's growing grass instead of cattle. I think we've whipped the technical part, to a certain extent. I think our problems are going to be more people problems. People keep expanding, more and more of them all the time. All I'm doing now is just going day-to-day and just fight the fires that are there today. It may be that it all works out. But it's going too difficult to maintain, in perpetuity, these big ranches. It's going to be difficult, also, to have an economic unit, in ranch country, if you don't have a lot of land. Maybe I'm too pessimistic, and every time it quits raining, I get pessimistic. If it rains and we get through this mountain of cattle that they claim we have by next fall, come back and my attitude will be a whole lot better.

Vaquillas Ranch Company

Interview with Gene Walker at the Barrel Springs Ranch, in Fort Davis, Texas, on August 7, 1998. Gene's father, James Oliver Walker Sr., started ranching in Laredo, Texas, in 1929. His two sons, Gene and J.O. Walker Jr., and daughter, Mary Elizabeth Quiros continue to operate the family ranch business with their families as well as their own independent ranches and businesses.

KJR: When did your father arrive in Loredo and start to ranch?

GW: Dad came to Laredo in 1910. He had been living in Louisiana and fell ill with malaria. They called it chills and fever but it was malaria. The doctors told him to get out to a dry country. It was just what the doctor ordered and the reason we wound up in Texas. He worked as a motorman on the streetcars in Laredo. He took different odd jobs and then, finally, got a foreman's job on a farm. Little by little, step by step he acquired enough capital to start ranching in 1929. I credit him for what we have today. He and my mother had to make the sacrifices that must be made to be in this business when starting from scratch.

GW: My father's credit was always good. So bankers were anxious to do business with him. We always owed money. Ten years after dad died we finished paying for all the land.

Since then, I've done the same thing. I acquired property I didn't have the money to buy, but under his reputation I got a good credit rating and was able to borrow and tackle large pieces of land on my own. I still owe half the banks in Texas, but that's my own and not a family obligation.

KJR: Was that unusual for that part of country?

GW: Yes it was. There was nothing, not even any hopes of any gas or oil where we were. It showed up in several places, which was a big help to us. What we have was not made from oil and gas — it was made with the cattle. The oil and gas have been nice; we've enjoyed it.

KJR: What is your cattle operation?

GW: We're a cow/calf operation all the way. We've always had commercial cattle but no registered cattle except bulls. We've always bought registered bulls. Our cow herd is a good grade of commercial cattle of most any breed. We have a little bit of everything. We use Beefmaster bulls predominantly

KJR: What has made your ranching operations successful?

GW: Lots of hard work, dedication and family unity. All that we have is by the grace of God. We work as a family and don't hire anything done that we can do ourselves. We're jacks of all trades. Labor is expensive and the biggest expense we have now. With the extra money from oil and gas we have done more improving the land by plowing and laying bigger and better tanks. We were already out of debt before we had any gas and oil. We each had separate land that we had acquired our own cattle and ourselves — we keep that separate.

GW: We all have cattle and land. Everybody's has to have a space and there are more and more people. That's why we know there's no more land. The truth of the matter is, that the population will double and triple and so forth. Even if he doesn't own it, he takes up some space, so that makes land more valuable.

KJR: What was the reason for expanding your ranching operations in west Texas? Is it different from your home ranch area in Laredo?

GW: We've had this place approximately five years now and the Wild Horse Ranch about two years. The land was more plentiful to buy here than at home. It was very difficult to acquire land of any size and adjoining property was even scarcer. The rainfall is the same here as it is at home. The terrain is what's different. The elevation is about five to six thousand feet higher here, consequently, around ten degrees cooler than South Texas on almost any given day of the year, winter and summer. This grass is very strong. Apparently it is stronger than it is at home. Cattle weigh a little heavier here at the same age. Grass has a lot to do with that and I suppose that the climate does too. We brought the cattle from South Texas and got them acclimated here.

KJR: What have you done differently than your father?

GW: I don't think there is anything in particular that he wouldn't have done himself if he had been here. We have changed from hard work say on horseback to easier physical work using machinery. Our operation now has grown almost exclusively with and by machines to gather cattle and to work them. All of that is done with machinery, where it used to be hard physical labor. New methods would come along and we snapped them up — from helicopters and airplanes to hydraulic chutes. My father would have embraced that I am sure, because he was that type of person.

KJR: So one of your business strategies is look out for what is new in technology or new approaches to making the labor less intensive and more efficient.

GW: That's right. I try to attend any and all meetings that pertain to the cattle business. My life is the cattle business. I travel all over the state, all over the United States and

sometimes out of the country. All hooked into the business. In a few weeks, I'm going to Australia and taking two of my grandchildren with me. My wife, Mary Kay, and I — she's deceased — we had begun to take one grandchild with us on these trips every year. I am continuing to do that.

KJR: Do you just see whatever you can and soak it up?
GW: Yes. Soak it up and try to learn it. There are many things that are thrown at you, or you pass by. I get a lot from a meeting, or a seminar, or seeing, or whatever. It is also important to learn what not to do as well as what to do.

KJR: What do you see for the future of the cattle industry?
GW: This drought is going to separate the men from the boys. Those who have been conservative and watched their P's and Q's and taken care, they'll pull through. We will see better times. I say "we" because I'm including myself in the bunch that's going to get through this crisis. I've been there before. I've seen times as bad, maybe even worse and was able to pull through then.

GW: Hopefully, we'll start eating more beef in this country. The consumption of beef has fallen off. Take, for instance, in Argentina their per capita consumption is 300 lbs. of beef a year. Here in the United States it's 60 some odd pounds. They seem to be doing very well by eating that much beef. There's not anything to the health concerns about beef. Human beings have eaten beef for thousands of years and I don't see any reason to quit.

GW: One of the main concerns of the consumer is that one steak will taste one way, or good, or medium, or bad. The next one will be different. They want consistency, so we must raise that type of beef and we will.

KJR: Is South Texas different from the rest of the state?

GW: Only in language. English is spoken exclusively anywhere in the state outside of South Texas, but that's about the only time that I notice a difference. When I went off to college at Texas Tech in Lubbock, I would miss the Spanish language because, I'd have no one to talk to. In South Texas we float back and forth in Spanish and English. They say if you know two languages, you're bilingual, if you know three languages, or even more, you're multi-lingual. If you know English only, then you're an American.

KJR: What would you advise young people, today, on how they could succeed in ranching?

GW: If you don't keep gaining experience and changing with the times pretty soon you'll get nipped in the bud. Ranching is a business. The way to stay successful is to always be curious. Ask your neighbors what they're doing. It all comes back to hard work. It's not a nine to five operation; it's twenty-four hours a day. You have to be willing to sacrifice, or you'd better do something else. Always ask for advice from someone that's obviously been in business longer than you have. I always believe that we can always learn something if you just let your mind open up.

KJR: Is there anything else that you would like to add?

GW: I would say that the importance of what our family has today and what we're doing is to be credited to my father, J.O. Walker, Sr. He and my mother made the sacrifice in order to have what they had and for their children. Of course, it takes a good woman for every successful man — there's always a good woman beside him. We worked hard too, but not like they did. We didn't have the worry and the stress that they did. We were just simply too young to realize how hard it really is. Until you get up and on your own and crises stares you in the face, that's when you realize how important the sacrifice that mom and dad made to acquire what we have.

KJR: What was the transition from your grandfather to your father's generation?

PW: Well, typically, because there wasn't any money, my grandfather couldn't really pay my dad that much to support a family. Instead he would give them a piece of land, or help them to get financing for a piece of land to run their own cows. Everyone was in debt all the time and there was a burden of that debt. Every time they'd come up for air, the creditors would know that they were good for it would loan more money. They would buy another ranch — take the raw land and turn it into something productive. They'd go back to fencing and water development and improve it so that they could operate it. My grandfather died in '64 having never been out of debt. His sons and son-in-law were still paying on the debt. They stopped buying. All they had in their mind was to get out of debt. That was their goal and they fought and scrimped and saved and got out of debt. About '74, they paid off the last ranch.

PW: We were really blessed that about 1977 natural gas was discovered on the ranch. With this new source of income we put money into ranch improvements.

KJR: Which family members are involved in the ranch today?

PW: My dad had four kids. Two boys and two girls. In our family I'm the oldest son. My wife Carllyn and I have four children. Rick, my brother, is the ranch pilot and takes care of probably a third of the ranch. He lives out at the home ranch with his wife, Jessica, and they have two children. My next sister is Elizabeth Owens and she lives in Alice, Texas. She's working in the family business but not on the ranch. Then, Kathleen Leindecker is my youngest sister and is in the family business, but not at the ranch.

PW: My dad's brother J.O. Walker Jr. married Bonnie Jean, who is deceased, and they had two children. He is retired and lives in San Antonio. His son Jim was working at the

ranch for probably fifteen years or so and has since moved into another area of the family business. His daughter Nancy was quite a hand on a horse. She was exceptional and didn't really like a saddle, she preferred to ride bareback. They called her a "little tick" because she rode so close to the horse, just like an Indian. She's working in the family business.

PW: My dad's sister, Mary Elizabeth Walker, married Evan B. Quiros, who for years was in charge of keeping books for the Vaquillas Ranch Company after their marriage. He's retired, or he says he's retired, but he's not. They had three children. His two daughters, Sadie and Quinnie, who are not involved in the family business. His son, Evan Quiros Jr., set up the ranch computer system. He worked at the ranch for probably 10 or 15 years himself, then he moved in to another part of the family business and he's managing that. My uncle was always worried about how the cattle business is tough and we need to get into something else, saying we could sell the land and put the money into stocks and bonds and get more income without even having to work. He was kidding, of course. So, what does he do when he retires? He buys him a little ranch. He's fighting it, dirt and drought and feed and thin cows, bad markets. Fifty years of belly aching and the first thing he does when he retires is buys a ranch for himself.

KJR: So everyone in the family is involved with the family business in one aspect or another?
PW: Yes. The family business began with my grandparents when they started the dairy farm, then the creamery, to the ranch. From the ranch we have diversified into other businesses, income producing entities.

PW: The family corporation is the Vaquillas Ranch Company. Originally it was the three siblings—my dad, his brother and sister. Typically, if just one was against something, nothing was done. They had to be in complete unity. That's worked very well. Now we are a family corporation with two members from each family branch on the board. But still, if somebody's adamant, the rest of the committee does not move forward until they research it further. I know you can get into problems by operating that way. One person can stop everything, but we haven't, yet.

KJR: How do you think you're preparing for the next century?
PW: We're still going to be in the stock business. I'm a stockman — I'll always be. Whether it's on the ranch or in Mexico or in Canada or in Australia, or Argentina, somewhere, I'm going to be fooling with cattle. Probably, more than likely my son will too. That's just our gift.

KJR: It sounds like ranching is in the Walker blood?
PW: We're definitely stockmen in our family. We're cattle people, like Abel. Cain was a farmer and Abel was a rancher. The stock market is not real. Everything is floating on paper or on computer screens. Dad is the main one in the family always pushing to buy land. Put your money in land.

PW: I am a stockman and then a cowboy. I have a gift. I can see cattle running and see the defects. I can sort them when they're running down the chute. I just pray right before, and I just see them and call them out and we cut them out of the herd. Of course, dad makes me identify what the defects are so that helps my diligence. It's not me. I'm not that good, I just ask for help and it just happens. We've got a pretty good cow herd. The same buyers buy your calves over the video, over national video every year, they like what they get, and they make them money. That's the main thing.

PW: We like other people to make lots of money. If you can help somebody produce something and make money, they'll always trade with you. All a man has to pass on is his honor. We only deal with honest people, people we can trust. If we have to worry about somebody, we just don't do it. If they are not going to be honest, we're just not going to

trade. We'll just do something else. Life's too short, staying up at night, trying to stay ahead, even though you might make more money with a quick deal, seemingly, but in the end it will crash and burn, along with him.

KJR: Ranching is a twenty-four hour a day business yet your grandfather, J.O. Walker Sr., would take Sundays off?

PW: Yes, he would try to shut the ranch down on Sundays. The human body is designed to run six days hard, hard as you want, but it has to stop one day. It doesn't have to be Sunday, but it has to be one day in seven. You actually get more production that way. God says to rest one day a week. My grandfather understood that and we do, too. We try to shut down one day a week the phones, everything and spend time with the Creator.

PW: The ranch is where our heart is. And hopefully for at least for another generation. What's amazing is that during the last decade in West Texas people are selling their ranches off after hundreds of years of ownership. There weren't any sales before that. Typically, the generation one goes in debt, the second one pays off the debt. Then the third generation enjoys the prosperity, they get lax and then their children, probably by the fourth and they don't care about any of the past.

KJR: What factors do you think makes your ranching operation successful?

PW: Diversification. In the '70's, we were probably the one of the first ranches to get on computer and of course everybody does it now. We're one of the first in South Texas to sell our cattle by video and precondition the calves. I guess we've been doing that for fifteen years or so. Also we've moved into more areas of the cattle business, importing and exporting of cattle, domestic buying and trading cattle. Our calves stay here in the U.S. We sell Mexican cattle — just steers, for grass and for feed lots. Hopefully, we've tried to diversify with international trading in real estate ranch buying and selling and trading.

PW: For all our success, we kid about our abundant blessings and successes. Whatever we get into, we seem to be successful. Folks say, "Well what are they doing?" We sit around and kid each other and say it's because we're so smart, but we know better. We give all the glory to God. There are a lot of people that work much harder and are more intelligent, and it just doesn't happen to them. We know it's not us. It's just a fact. My grandfather was a believer in Jesus Christ, and his beliefs have passed down through the generations. Of course, not everybody in the family believes as strongly. He blessed our grandfather and that blessing is still being poured out on his descendants.

Williams Ranches

Interview with Clayton and Modesta Williams at their corporate headquarters Claydesta, in Midland, Texas, on July 22, 1998. Today the Williams Ranches include five ranches and a farming operation, along with other business ventures. Clayton and Modesta have five children total: Kelvie Muhlbauer, Allyson Groner, and Clayton Wade, Jeff and Chicora Williams.

KJR: Did you both grow up on ranches in Texas?
CW: We both did. My family came to Fort Stockton in 1883. My grandfather surveyed the town of Lubbock, but he was not a rancher. He was a lawyer and a surveyor and an entrepreneur. My family had a ranch and that was my love. I grew up, cowboyed, farmed, irrigated, and went to A&M to study animal husbandry. That was my degree. I intended to be a rancher. While I was in the army, my dad sold the ranch and leased the farm. I was out of work. This was the best thing that ever happened because we didn't have that much of a ranch, it was very poor country. Having a "want to" in my blood and ranching in my blood I always wanted a better and bigger ranch. I didn't have one, didn't have the money. When I met Modesta and her family, fine cattle people in Borden County, they had an old-line ranch north of Big Springs. We clicked and she loved the ranching. She

didn't hold me back when I wanted to buy a ranch. We were fortunate that I didn't inherit a ranch, although Modesta inherited part of hers.

MW: I grew up on the ranch. We lived in town during the school year, would go back to the ranch every weekend. I was a cowgirl and I rodeoed some. I was never real, real good at it — I mean professional at it. But we loved it and it was a good place for kids. My grandfather came to West Texas in 1900 and he worked for Colonel C.C. Slaughter, as a cowboy. Colonel Slaughter's cowboys would go out and homestead. My granddaddy was one of those cowboys. Through the years he decided that maybe that was a good idea and so then he started putting together the ranch that we have right now. He home-steaded some land and started buying land from cowboys that surrounded him. This was about 1900. We're a cow/calf operation. When I was growing up my granddaddy was a yearling man. He was of the last fellows that drove the cattle to Lamesa where the train loaded them up and railed them up to Kansas City, or wherever. Today, of course, you have all of the modernized big trucks or you own your own trucks.

KJR: Do you remember the cattle drives?
MW: I have a picture over at my mother's house and the other day my aunt was visiting and she said, "You know, you were on that cattle drive." I said, "I was not." She said that it was the last cattle drive from our ranch to Lamesa, and my mother was pregnant with me and she was riding. It was such a neat thing that she knew because her husband, my mother's brother was on that drive. Actually, I get a little emotional about this story. The drive was about twenty to twenty-five miles going right down the draws through the countryside and stopping at night.

CW: I was fortunate that I made some money. When I made some money, then I wanted to buy a ranch. The trouble was I was never able to quit buying, and that kept me broke in ranches. We make money — we're probably not going to make any money this year. We have a real operation. You won't see any white fences. I enjoy it thoroughly. I'm a conservationist. I've fought the brush, I've tried to improve the pastures, and I've

increased the productivity. I love the land. I love to make the land productive. We're in the desert so you can better utilize your country when you have more water. I've used pipelines, electric pumps. I've done a lot of spreading of water. I've done a pretty good job of it. I like to do it in conjunction with nurturing more game.

MW: When we went out to Alpine, Clayton started his water spreading. The old-time ranchers out there just couldn't believe what he was doing. He did a beautiful job of clearing the brush, built all the dikes and water outlets. I helped him do a little bit of that, and it made beautiful pastures.

CW: I use rotation grazing, where I can, where it fits. It's a modified form. I use the general practices of root plowing, reseeding, fire — I used to burn. I fenced the rough country off the flats, to utilize the rough country. If you don't, the cows will starve to death on the flat before they'll get in the rough rocks and mountains. We run a cow/calf and a yearling operation. We produce a lot of good cattle. We have a good calf crop. We have five ranches. I own three, my wife owns part of one, and we lease from her family. Frequently, I lease ranches from other people.

KJR: With all of your diverse business how do you find time to work on the ranch?
CW: I spend a lot of time in the office and many times I think I'm so busy; I shouldn't spend three days gathering cattle, branding or shipping, or whatever we're doing. The minute that I manage to get out of bed and get on horseback at daylight, I'm just as happy as I can be. That's something that's never left. I like to be in the pen. I like to do it. I think if you're going to own a ranch, you should be part of it. That's my view, because I grew up doing that as a boy. Also, I have good men and most of them have been with me a long time. Laughingly I tell them they either can't get a job somewhere else, or I'm overpaying them, because they've been with me a long time.

MW: Clayton and I love both love the ranching. When we go out to the ranch — either to Borden County or to Alpine — it seems like a weight is lifted off our shoulders. Those are our two loved places. My ranch being my homeland. Alpine because we bought it only a few years after we got married. That was "our" ranch. There was not a formal road, just a winding trail up through the ranch. We have built everything out there. We built it together with our kids. We call it a 'Happy Cove' because there are so many happy times out there. Borden County is a little different from Alpine. In Borden County, that's a smaller ranch, but they do a lot of neighboring. Each neighbor goes over and works at another's ranch when it's time to work cattle, or ship, doctor or whatever they might need. In Alpine, the ranches are probably larger and you have more hired help; so you just don't neighbor like you do over in Borden County.

KJR: What about your cattle business?
CW: Basically, we have bred Brangus. At this point, I'm probably taking a little ear off the Brangus. I'm putting Angus bulls on my Brangus cows. We were in the Registered Brangus business, a real good one for 20 years. It was a very profitable period of time. During that time the market was demanding larger cattle. We got them bigger and bigger until we got them too big. As a result, the yearlings keep growing instead of fattening, and they required 145 days in the feed lot instead of 120 or 125. That is another reason for increasing the Angus percentage, to pare down a bit on size while improving beef quality. I'll have a herd that's 18-3/4% Brahman and 81-1/4% Angus. It's nearly all Angus, but I still retain most of the good qualities of the Brahman...

KJR: What about the cattle industry today?
CW: We've become such efficient producers, as have the farmers, in our country, that we're producing bigger animals, more of them, better conversion. All the things they taught us to do in college, how to be a better producer. We've made real improvements in beef production today. We're awash in beef — we've done it to ourselves in a way by being so efficient.

CW: Ranching people will ranch, and it has nothing to do with profitability, because they enjoy it. There's an attachment to owning land. There's a security to land, there's the love of the land, and there's the ego of the land. All these emotions come in. People buy land and get no return or one percent return, and they are as happy as they can be. If my wife had money in the stock market that didn't make two or three percent, she wouldn't be happy at all!

CW: As far as the beef, I'm trying not to go broke, as everybody else is during this drought. We had some rain, but there's so little that these people can do. It's a lot easier for me because I have some income unlike somebody that makes their living one-hundred percent from ranching. It let's me put in capital. I can put those extra water troughs to utilize the land better. I can put a fence for rotation grazing cause I have the money to do it. You can't do these things if you don't make the money in the first place. We've had seven dry years and low prices. Most of the ranchers that lease ranches can make a good return, if they got a good lease and if they get rain. Now one of the keys to ranching is knowing when to quit and you need some help from the Lord there. Sometimes you need to downsize. I sold half my herd. I follow the commodities. I watch the board. I watch the cycles.

KJR: You're a buyer of beef, a consumer, with a household of kids to feed, as well as being a woman rancher. What do you think the industry needs to do?
MW: I think that we have to get out and just pump our beef. Tell the consumer how good and healthy it is. One thing that has absolutely helped us probably as much as anything in the last year is Dr. Robert C. Atkins diet. Clayton is on that diet and he has done so well. I think it starts with the fact that everyone wants to be healthy. It's everyone wanting to look trim and slim. When they find out that beef is not what's making them fat, it's the sugar and the carbohydrates. Once they realize this we might make some progress.

CW: *Dr. Atkins' New Diet Revolution* book shows scientific studies suggesting that every primitive culture, once they introduce sugar to their diet, have heart attacks 20 years later. When you read Atkin's statistics you say that everybody is crazy who lives on low fat diets. Paul Dudley White was Eisenhower's heart surgeon and he said he never saw any heart trouble until the '20's. Why was that? Because our ancestors had a farm and they had milk, cream, and butter, and eggs, and beef, and pork. They had a few vegetables but mostly protein. There was no heart attack then. It is tied to insulin. When you eat sugar or refined carbohydrates, which are bread and corn and what have you, you trigger that insulin and it wants to grab everything it can and convert it to fat. If you don't give the body sugar or carbohydrates it won't do that.

CW: In my own case, my blood sugar has dropped dramatically — which I could never get down before. I even quit taking my cholesterol medication and it is still low. My good cholesterol is up for the first time since I've been going to doctors. That's because I'm eating beef and eggs for breakfast with bacon, and I just don't eat the sugar. This shift in understanding is one hope for the cattle business. Since consumers have gone the 'healthy' low fat diet, the weight of America has gone up 27%. People have thought that chicken and fish are healthy. The chicken they're selling you is about 30 or 40% bone. You take the chicken breast or drumstick and check the amount of meat with the bone. With beef you're getting one-hundred percent meat generally, unless you get a T-bone. So beef is cheaper than what it appears and the housewife is fooled, which surprises me a little bit.

KJR: With perception being reality today, how do you change that perception?
CW: I think we're poor marketers. The main thing is that the propaganda against the cattle industry and beef by the health community. It has been destructive for us. As an industry we have not gotten the facts out there that contradicts their propaganda.

KJR: What legacy would you like to leave for future generations?

CW: I think my legacy will be in my land improvement, where I've grown more grass and less brush. Taking the water and instead of letting it run away I've spread it out. I think in some of my practices I've been innovative by putting the water in the high, rough country and using it with live cattle where it was not usable before. I like things to produce. I like them to be of value. I like to keep the game. I fight the mountain lions all the time because they're killing deer. They'll kill two or three deer a week sometimes. I like the quail, I enjoy them. I'm even conserving jackrabbits, of all things. There's a balance in nature and when you ranch in the desert, or anywhere you have to deal with it. So my legacy is a better ranching practice to make the land productive, complement it with quail and deer and javelinas. I'd like my kids to hold onto it, but that depends on them, not me.

CW: One of the weaknesses of ranching is repeating the past — my dad did it that way and my granddad did it that way, so I will. I've taught school — I'm a teacher, I'm teaching my people. I use the ranch road as an analogy: The old boy started out on the first road, when he had a car. He started driving and he saw a cow and blew the horn. Oh, damn, I have to check that out and he drove over to it. Then he's with a girlfriend and he hits a bump and dodges a creek. If building this road were your goal, you'd have created a straight line. Well, he wandered all over in that car. Life's like this because 'they did it that way.' What did the next guy do? He followed that road because there were already tracks there. So following condemns you to make the mistakes that your ancestor did, and maybe they didn't put that road in the best place first of all. I question every-thing. I evaluate it — if it's good I'll do it, and if it's not, I'll do something different. I've never felt confined because somebody did it that way before. In fact I'm probably a little bit of a rebel. If they did it, I wonder if there is a better way to do it.

Acknowledgments

This book is one of the most personal projects I have undertaken. It was a remarkable experience to sit across from each one of these ranchers in the midst of such difficult times. They were always gracious and extremely generous. Special thanks to Al Micallef for having the vision to publish this second book. A loving thanks to all the ranchers: Rob and Peggy Brown and family, Tom and Becky Moorhouse, John Moorhouse, Jimmie and Nancy Powell, Primo and Carllyn Walker, Nolan and Ruth Ryan, Clayton and Modesta Williams, Dub Waldrip and Jim McAdams, Tom and Pat Woodward, Jon and Jackie Means, J.J. Gibson, Mike and Shonda Gibson, Bob Hudgins and Jim and James McAllen.

Thank you to Joye Turner, who learned more about Texas ranching while transcribing the interview tapes than she dreamed possible. A special thanks to Heidi Hause for her support on all the project coordination; Mike Micallef, Sue Stephenson, Cathy Snoddy, and Mike Evans at JMK.

My love to Fred Boeger and gratitude for his love and patience. I am abundantly blessed with friends, old and new, who took me into heart and home: Carla Curry and Gary Lovelady, Joan Roulac-Torrence, Mischel Denise Whitehead, Jan Lea, Elna Iversen, Beth and Sherry McNutt, Kristen and Bob Tallman, Jody and Douglas Lindemann and Chuck and Betty Weeth.

Blessing to you all, **Kathleen Jo Ryan**